Mill

GUIDES FOR THE PERPLEXED

Guides for the Perplexed are clear, concise, and accessible introductions to thinkers, writers, and subjects that students and readers can find especially challenging. Concentrating specifically on what it is that makes the subject difficult to grasp, these books explain and explore key themes and ideas, guiding the reader toward a thorough understanding of demanding material.

Guides for the Perplexed available from Bloomsbury:

A GUIDE FOR THE PERPLEXED

Mill

SUJITH KUMAR

BLOOMSBURY

LONDON • NEW DELHI • NEW YORK • SYDNEY

Bloomsbury Academic
An imprint of Bloomsbury Publishing Plc

50 Bedford Square
London
WC1B 3DP
UK

175 Fifth Avenue
New York
NY 10010
USA

www.bloomsbury.com

First published 2013

British Library Cataloguing-in-Publication Data
A catalogue record for this book is available from the British Library.

ISBN: HB: 978-1-8470-6402-8
PB: 978-1-8470-6403-5

Library of Congress Cataloging-in-Publication Data
Kumar, Sujith.
Mill: a guide for the perplexed/Sujith Kumar.
p. cm. – (Guides for the perplexed)
Includes bibliographical references (p.) and index.
ISBN 978-1-84706-402-8 (hardcover: alk. paper) – ISBN 978-1-84706-403-5
(pbk.: alk. paper) – ISBN 978-1-4411-9299-8 (ebook pdf: alk. paper) –
ISBN 978-1-4411-9110-6 (ebook epub: alk. paper) 1. Mill, John Stuart,
1806-1873. I. Title.
B1607.K86 2012
192–dc23
2012015687

Typeset by Deanta Global Publishing Services, Chennai, India
Printed and bound in India

CONTENTS

PREFACE

Mill has not yet entered the public consciousness like some other philosophers of his stature. Apart from Monty Python, no musician I know of has worked him into their song lyrics, or been arrested with a copy of one his essays. Mill's arguments do sometimes find their way into a legal opinion, or into a newspaper's editorial, but most people familiar with his work probably first encountered him at university. Mill's best known writings, *Utilitarianism* and *On Liberty* are usually presented to undergraduates as paradigmatic examples of utilitarian ethics, and arguments for liberalism, even though these essays are from being so one-dimensional. Mill is certainly an important figure in these traditions, but the real genius of his thought is the synthesis of disparate philosophical traditions, such as German Romanticism, French Positivism, and British Empiricism. In important ways, Mill's eclectic doctrine prefigures the central features of the British Idealism of T. H. Green, Bernard Bosanquet, or the New Liberalism of L. T. Hobhouse. Today, the dominant strands of liberal thought differ from Mill's doctrine in crucial respects, but recent contributions to perfectionism, especially that of Joseph Raz, still share many affinities.

Mill may have articulated his moral and political doctrine over 150 years ago, but Mill is not merely a figure in the history of Anglo-American thought. His enduring importance is based on the fact that the issues he addresses are very much alive, making his relevance to politics today manifest. Whether delineating the limits of free speech, or assessing harm to others in the public realm, the only thing unusual about Mill's participation in these current debates is how well-argued his position would be, compared to the media pundits and politicians who are now the principle exponents. Applying Mill's principls to contemporary problems is not only appropriate, but in many cases illuminating. His applicability to our time is not just because of the ubiquity of some key political and social problems, but also due to his ability to cut through the superficial and temporal trappings of a problem, and address its heart. This book is therefore a modest contribution to the effort to maintain interest in this influential and challenging thinker. Much interpretive controversy surrounds his writings. My aim is in part to answer some questions about Mill, but more so to continue to spur new ones.

Many people have helped in the completion of this project, but I would like to pay special thanks to Professor Richard Matthews for bringing me to this point in my life, and commenting on drafts of this project. I must also thank my wife, Sandra, for all of her moral support. Lastly, I want to thank the kind employees at Bloomsbury for their patience.

CHAPTER ONE

Introduction

Biographical sketch

For people of great accomplishments, it is only natural to question the details of their personal lives. To know what events fueled their ambitions or shaped the character of their minds is a fair direction of inquiry, not only for historians, but for anyone wanting to contextualize their accomplishments. In the case of philosophers, such personal information might even illuminate key elements of their thought, or guide interpretation. The lives of some philosophers actually *beg* this kind of inquiry. Was Nietzsche's alleged syphilis related to his powerfully subversive ideas? Perhaps. John Stuart Mill is another thinker whose personal life draws much lay and scholarly attention, in part because of his own intentions. Born on 20 May 1806, Mill's life is now firmly enshrined in popular lore. The Collected Works of John Stuart Mill contains 32 volumes of essays, newspaper articles, speeches, letters, and diary entries, the very first of which is his *Autobiography*. Published just after Mill's death in 1873, the Autobiography is as much a carefully considered work for a wide audience as it is an honest account of his life. In other words, it needs to be taken with a grain of salt. Mill clearly is intent to explain and justify certain controversial details of his life and work, and so the *Autobiography* could serve as *his* road map to our exploration of his thought (Capadli 2004, p. xiii). At the same time, his Autobiography could also fittingly be placed at the end of the *Collected Works*, because it also stands as a fascinating case study of some of his central theories. Throughout his writings, Mill is concerned with the concept of character. He never systematically defines character, but as one of the primary determinants of behavior, he focuses on it as his strategy of reform. To that end, he lays the groundwork for a science of character formation, called ethology. Mill ultimately fails to establish the science, and yet his own early upbringing can be viewed as a case study in the development of ethological principles (Ball 2000, p. 33). However the *Autobiography* stands in relation to his other works, certain details of his life are undeniably relevant to his arguments, and so a brief sketch will serve the reader in this introduction to the challenging topics in Mill's thought.

Educational experiment and mental crisis

John Stuart Mill was born in 1806 to James and Harriet Mill in London. James Mill was educated at the University of Edinburgh and moved to London in 1802 to become a writer. By the time John was born, James had become associated with the Philosophic Radicals, a group of social reformers whose aim was to promote the greatest happiness for the greatest numbers, or utility, with their policy reforms. Such a standard was indeed quite radical, because norms, morals, and even policy were typically determined by ambiguous standards, such as tradition, intuition, scripture, or the interests of the Aristocracy. For example, the Philosophic Radicals worked to overturn the Corn Laws, which prohibited the importation of grains, much to the enrichment of the landed aristocracy (Miller 2010, p. 5). James Mill along with the leader of the Philosophic Radicals, Jeremy Bentham, were exponents of Classical Utilitarianism, which holds that pleasure is the only good and pain the only evil. In addition to serving as a moral standard, pain and pleasure were also powerful motivators of action. For the Radicals, knowing people's sensitivities to pleasure and pain was all that was necessary in order to reform institutions so that people's interests overlapped, and could be maximized in harmony.

James Mill taught John at home, where he had an extremely regimented and rigorous education. John was learning Ancient Greek by age three, was teaching Latin to his younger siblings by age eight, and was editing his father's *History of India* by age eleven. John was well on his way to becoming a towering intellectual by his early teens, which attracted the attention of associates of the

Philosophic Radicals, such as the historian George Grote and the economist David Ricardo. Although John was already studying law under the legal scholar, John Austin, he had somewhat of an epiphany in 1821, when he was introduced to Bentham's *Traité de Législation*.

> When I laid down the last volume of the *Traité* I had become a different being. The 'principle of utility', understood as Bentham understood it, and applied in the manner in which he applied it through these three volumes, fell exactly into its place as the keystone which held together the detached and fragmentary component parts of my knowledge and beliefs. It gave unity to my conceptions of things. I now had opinions; a creed, a doctrine, a philosophy: in one among the best senses of the word, a religion; the inculcation and diffusion of which could be made the principal outward purpose of a life. (Mill 1981, p. 68)

By his late teens, John was an active member of the Philosophic Radicals, publishing their *Westminster Review*, and participating in the London Debating Society. James Mill worked for the East India Company, and he was able to secure employment for John there in 1823, who was a mere 17-year-old. Upon reflecting on his own upbringing, Mill recognized how extraordinary it was. In fact, Mill concluded that the experiment of his own education proved the inadequacies of customary education, and that young pupils were capable of developing their minds much sooner than in early adulthood. Mill makes clear that his father did not drill facts into his mind with an "education of cram," which had the effect of crippling the faculties of the mind, rather than developing them. Instead, John was forced to think for himself and figure out solutions by his own means. His father only provided assistance once it was clear that John had exhausted himself. Even though Mill was kept apart from other children, and appears not have had any childhood friends, he reports bearing no resentment toward his father for the totalitarian childhood he experienced (Mill 1981, p. 35).

Mill was well on his way to becoming the leader of the next generation of Radical reformers of English society. His career in the East India Company was progressing well, and he was motivated by Bentham's utilitarian creed. He had a purpose in life—to bring about all of the reforms of the movement, and he had come to identify his own happiness with this end. But by the autumn of 1826, Mill found himself in a "dull state of nerves," unable to enjoy the activities he once did (Mill 1981, p. 137). And then the cruelest of all ironies befell upon this paragon of utilitarian thought. He asked himself, "Suppose that all your objects in life were realized; that all the changes in institutions and opinions which you are looking forward to, could be completely effected at this very instant: would this be a great joy and happiness to you?" And an irrepressible self-consciousness distinctly answered, "No!" (Mill 1981, p. 139).

Mill fell into depression at the realization that his own happiness would not be included in the utilitarian goal of general happiness. Not even his normal remedies of sleeping or reading were able to lift his spirits. James Mill was the last person he could speak to about his condition, because John did not want his father to think that the great pedagogical experiment of his life was a failure, and he doubted his father's ability to sympathize. As for John's mother, she is conspicuously absent from the Autobiography. Sadly, John states plainly that had he felt love for any person, he would not have been in such a state (Mill 1981, p. 139). Mill summarizes his grief with lines from Samuel Taylor Coleridge's Dejection, an Ode:

A grief without a pang, void, dark and drear,
A drowsy, stifled, unimpassioned grief,
Which finds no natural outlet or relief
In word, or sigh, or tear (Ibid.)

Apparently, the great experiment did not include development of the emotional faculties. The Radicals' embrace of the psychological laws of associationism implied that any activity or goal could become attached to one's own happiness, and James Mill constantly encouraged John to associate his own pleasure only with the most laudable of pursuits. But instead of helping John to develop and broaden the capacity for happiness, his father "trusted altogether to the old familiar instruments, praise and blame, reward and punishment" (Mill 1981, p. 141). Mill had been instilled with such an analytical mind that he could not help but analyze away the tenuous associations he had made with his own happiness. Analysis was a powerful tool that could bring clarity to obscurity, connect the seemingly unrelated, and reveal both cause and effect. But without developed emotional capacities, all of the labored associations between valuable desires and happiness could be dissolved. In short, James had created an analytical machine that was incapable of feeling genuinely happy.

John's stupor lasted for about six months, until one day when he was reading the French historian, Jean François Marmontel's *Memoirs*, he came across the passage where Marmontel recounts the death of his father and how the family mourned sorrowfully. John was struck by Marmontel's inspiration (at the time still a child) to replace his father in the family and provide all that he did for them. What happened next is best stated by John himself, "A vivid conception of the scene and its feelings came over me, and I was moved to tears. From this moment my burthen grew lighter" (Mill 1981, p. 145). By vicariously experiencing his father's death, John was able to pull himself slowly out of his depression. His emotional capacities had not been entirely destroyed by his analytical abilities, and he was able to feel not happiness, but "cheerfulness," again (Mill 1981, p. 145). John admits that his mental crisis resulted in two important changes to his thinking. First, despite his crisis, John never doubted that happiness was the sole end in life, but now he was convinced that happiness could not be attained by directly aiming for it. People should pursue various ends for themselves, and enjoy the happiness that comes with them. Second, whereas the utilitarianism of Bentham accepted individuals as they were, and sought to maximize happiness by rearranging their external relationships with each other, John now understood that the greatest happiness to be had was by attending to the "internal culture" of individuals (Mill 1981, p. 147). No longer content to merely satiate people's capacities for pleasure, he now aimed to expand and refine people's capacities for pleasure. As will be discussed in the next few chapters, these are crucial revisions to the Classical Utilitarianism of Bentham.

New thought and Harriet

By the late 1820s, John had fully recovered from his malaise and was ready to explore his new revisions to the utilitarian doctrine. He continued participating in the London Debating Society, and there he was introduced to French Positivism in the writings of Saint-Simon and Auguste Comte. Like the Philosophic Radicals, the Positivists were trying to apply the logic and rationality of the natural sciences to the business of reforming society. Where the Radicals differed was with the ahistorical and universalist ambition underpinning their thought. The Positivists, on the other hand, understood human knowledge and civilization to be moving through history in stages, each with its own appropriate mode of social and political organizing. Also through the Society, John would meet John Sterling, with whom John Mill would become very close until Sterling's death in 1844. In his words, "With Sterling I soon became very intimate, and was more attached to him than I have ever been to any other man" (Mill 1981, p. 161). Sterling had studied the work of the German Romantic Philosopher, Friedrich von Schelling, and eventually introduced John to the writings of the English Romantic poet, Samuel Coleridge. Through their English interlocutors, Mill would come to absorb much German Idealism and Romanticism into his own thought. Late German Romanticism provided exactly the counter balance to Classical Utilitarianism that John was seeking. Whereas for the utilitarians, the solution for social problems was to be found in altering the external relationships between individuals, the Romantics sought the solution to the crisis of the Enlightenment in the concept of *bildung*, or self-development. Broadly speaking, the Romantics acknowledged the human need for liberty, but also understood that individuals were culturally and historically embedded and that there was no universal or abstract perspective. In order to reconcile the competing demands of liberty and society, they focused on "fullest, richest, and most harmonious development of the potentialities of the individual, the community, or the human race" (Burrow 1969, p. xviii). Through the Society, and the various salons of his growing social circle, John's intellectual horizons were expanding as he was meeting thinkers of all different sorts, and was being introduced to ideas from all over the Continent. By 1836, both Bentham and his father had passed away, and John (henceforth Mill) was free to develop his revised utilitarianism. He never renounced Benthamism, and continued to champion the causes of the Philosophic Radicals, primarily by continuing to run the Westminster Review, but Mill was now free to revise his inherited utilitarianism, which, as will be discussed, may have constituted a break from it. Mill's primary aim, at this point, was to combine the utilitarianism of Bentham with the Romanticism of Coleridge (Capaldi 2004, p. 89).

By far, the most influential person Mill meets during this period, at least according to him, was Harriet Taylor. Harriet was married to John Taylor and confessed to a mutual friend, William Fox that she was frustrated by her husband's intellectual inadequacies (Miller 2010, p. 8). This was arguably very convenient for Fox because earlier, Mill was attracted to Eliza Flower and had even asked her to marry him. Ms Flower, who was in love with Fox (who was himself married) refused Mill's proposal. It is 'plausible' that Fox introduced Harriet to Mill as much to occupy Mill's affections, as to help out Harriet (Capaldi 2004, p. 102). Whatever the case may have been, the two were immediately smitten with each other. As John puts it:

> Up to the time when I first saw her, her rich and powerful nature had chiefly unfolded itself according to the received type of feminine genius. To her outer circle she was a beauty and a wit, with an air of natural distinction, felt by all who approached her: to the inner, a woman of deep and strong feeling, of penetrating and intuitive intelligence, and of an eminently meditative and poetic nature. (Mill 1981, p. 192)

Mill spends pages of the *Autobiography* gushing over the beauty and virtue of Harriet, and claiming her intellect to be far superior to his. Shortly after their introduction, Mill began to spend most evenings with the Taylors, until it became obvious to all of England that Mill and Harriet had developed feelings for each other. Despite their insistence that the relationship was purely platonic, it was hugely scandalous and drew the disapproval of many of Mill's family and close associates (including James Mill up until his death). Despite the awkwardness of the relationships, Harriet continued to live with Taylor (though no longer sharing a bed with him) and cared for him right up to his death in 1849. John Stuart Mill and Harriet Taylor finally married in 1851, thereby creating the *second* Mrs Harriet Mill (the first one being John's mother) and moved to the Blackheath area of London, largely keeping to themselves.

By this time, Mill had published *A System of Logic* and *Principles of Political Economy*, and so he had established himself as a public intellectual. Mill continued to work at the East India Company until it was nationalized in 1858. That was also the same year that Harriet died, as the two were traveling in France. During their brief time together, the two of them collaborated on a number of essays together, including Mill's best known work, *On Liberty*.

Mill claims that with the addition of her thoughts, the essay was "a kind of philosophic textbook of a single truth," of the importance of providing a sphere of liberty for "human nature to expand itself in innumerable and conflicting directions" (Mill 1981, p. 259). The extent of Harriet's contribution to *On Liberty*, as well as to other works, is a matter of dispute, largely because she published so little under her own name (Miller 2010, p. 10). Regardless of her actual contribution, Mill certainly felt that she deserved part authorship, as his eulogy to her at the start of the essay makes clear.

> To the beloved and deplored memory of her who was the inspirer, and in part the author, of all that is best in my writings —the friend and wife whose exalted sense of truth and right was my strongest incitement, and whose approbation was my chief reward—I dedicate this volume. Like all that I have written for many years, it belongs as much to her as to me; but the work as it stands has had, in a very insufficient degree, the inestimable advantage of her revision . . . Were I but capable of interpreting to the world one half the great thoughts and noble feelings which are buried in her grave, I should be the medium of a greater benefit to it, than is ever likely to arise from anything that I can write, unprompted and unassisted by her all but unrivaled wisdom. (Mill 1977b, p. 216)

Mill thought that the essay would be one his best known works after his lifetime, and he was, of course, absolutely correct on this point. *On Liberty* is one of the best examples of the German Romantic influence on Mill's thought, especially that of Wilhelm von Humboldt. Interestingly, there is only one passing reference to utility in the essay, even though there are several places where invoking it would help clarify certain ideas. Humboldt is the only writer mentioned in a positive light in the essay more than once and an excerpt from his *The Limits of State Action* shares top billing with Harriet's eulogy at the beginning of *On Liberty*.

Parliament and the maturity of utilitarianism

After Harriet's death, Mill split his time between London and Avignon, where she was buried. Harriet's youngest daughter, Helen, had replaced her as Mill's assistant and companion, and he adored her as his own daughter, lavishing her with almost as much praise as her mother. Helen was active in the women's rights movement, and Mill's arguments for legal and social equality between men and women are found in the somewhat unpolished, *The Subjection of Women*, published in 1869. At the time women could not own property, vote, or apply for divorce. These legal inequalities lead to womens' dependence on men for their very subsistence, and Mill argued that this deformed their characters. On the one hand, Mill was very progressive for his time, arguing for full legal equality between men and women, on the other hand, he also claimed that women's primary responsibilities should be domestic labor. Mill was a Liberal Member of Parliament from 1865 to 1868 representing Westminster, and he attempted to amend the Reform Bill of 1867 to extend the vote to women. He was ultimately unsuccessful, but Mill championed several progressive and controversial causes, like home rule for the Irish, an inheritance tax on the wealthy estates, and he even tried to introduce a system of single transferable voting, created by Thomas Hare. Throughout his time in Parliament, Mill was a champion of the working classes he represented. But as the demographics of his constituency were changing, the electorate was becoming less receptive to his positions, and Mill ultimately lost his bid for reelection in 1868. (Capaldi 2004, p. 330). Mill was a private citizen and again, and he withdrew to a small flat in Westminster, where he continued publishing and maintaining his many letter correspondences.

The 1860s also saw the publication of some Mill's now best-known writings, such as *Considerations on Representative Government*, and two lengthy critiques of Sir William Hamilton and Auguste Comte. Arguably the most important publication at this time was the definitive statement of his moral theory in the essay, *Utilitarianism*. Originally published in three parts in Fraser's Magazine in 1861, it was Mill's attempt to defend his reformed utilitarian creed against critics of the Radicals, such as Thomas Babington Macaulay and Thomas Carlyle. They were critical of the impoverished conception of human nature as simple pleasure-seekers that the Radicals took as the premise of their policies. Motivated by the German Romantics, and armed with the principles of associationist psychology developed by his father, Mill argues that individuals are capable of developing their capacities to experience higher qualities of pleasure, and that the standard of happiness in no way precluded the disinterest pursuit of virtue. The longest discussion on the essay is his account of justice. Much of customary morality overlapped with utilitarian morality, and so Mill needed to account for the fact that the standard of happiness could justify moral principles, and was not simply a doctrine of mere expediency. As a committed utilitarian all of his life, this essay forms the foundation of all of Mill's social and political writings. Mill was a reformer first, and a philosopher and social theorist second. His writings are largely polemical, concerned primarily to argue a specific thesis, or to attack someone else's. Two questions surround the legacy of his work: first can his moral and political prescriptions be justified in a utilitarian framework, and second, is his doctrine of thought empirically sustainable. Mill was a committed empiricist all of his life. As such, only observation and experience can confirm the legitimacy of his claims. The rationalist and intuitionist moralists that Mill criticized were not burdened by banalities, such as the real world. Being derived from pure reason or a moral faculty of the mind, such thinkers needed only to articulate their principles. The standards for Mill, set by his own epistemological and methodological commitments, are much higher—the only true test is the implementation of his principles and observation of the outcomes. The complexity of his thought, and the fact that all of his reform efforts were intended as deductions from the standard of general happiness make this test difficult to conduct. Despite being denied this ultimate vindication, Mill was a hugely influential thinker in his own lifetime, and remains central figure in the disparate traditions of utilitarianism, liberalism, and English Romanticism. Mill died in May of 1873. He was, of course, buried next to Harriet in Avignon. But a statue of Mill remains at the very edge of Westminster, at the Temple Gardens, where he continues to look over not only the seat of British Government, but over the entire spirit of governing in the United Kingdom.

Structure of this presentation

This presentation of Mill's thought is directed primarily at the advanced university student, early graduate student, or lay reader familiar with the topics and vocabulary of political thought. It is intended not as a comprehensive overview of Mill's corpus, but as an introduction to the topics in Mill's thought that are particularly challenging to access on their own. As such, it is selective. I have excluded many important areas of thought worthy of examination, and have glossed over many of the controversies surrounding his ideas, but in so doing hope to provide a more concise overview of Mill's liberal-utilitarian doctrine of reform. Each chapter is sufficiently self-contained to be read on its own, but taken together, I consider this book to be a contribution to the revisionary literature in Millian scholarship that has developed in the last 40 years. The traditional critique of Mill is directed primarily at his liberal-utilitarian project and begins with Mill's contemporary, James Fitzjames Stephen, in his *Liberty, Equality, and Fraternity*, and runs largely through Sir Isaiah Berlin (1996), Gertrude Himmelfarb (1974), and C. L. Ten (1980). The common strand running through their criticisms is the argument that it is incoherent to build a system of individual rights justified and mediated by a prior commitment to maximizing utility, because the two pull in opposite directions. For example, it might be to the greatest good for the greatest numbers to violate the rights of a particular minority of the community. In response, there has been a revisionary effort to rescue the coherency of Mill's project found in the writings of Rees (1996), Berger, (1984), Gray (1996), Riley (1998), and Miller (2010), among many others. These works are primarily interpretive, employing several of Mill's other writings to interpret his liberal-utilitarian project in such a way as to make it coherent. This particular contribution to the revisionary literature of Mill's project is influenced by the writings of Donner (1991) and Habibi (2001) who stress the centrality of self-development in Mill's ethics. John Gray's attribution of indirect utilitarianism has been influential in my understanding of Mill's project (although I do not use the term here), along with his highlighting the theory of progress that underpins all of Mill's writings. Finally, Joseph Hamburger's (1999) subversive—yet ultimately unsustainable—attribution of Illiberal intentions to Mill has also influenced my interpretation. The topics in this book are wider than those covered in most revisionary efforts, and so I also want to highlight F. W. Garforth's (1979) book length study on detailing Mill's thoughts on education, and Fred Wilson (1990) critical assessment of Mill's psychological theories, as also informing my understanding of Mill's thought. In light of the tension between utility and rights, any argument for coherency in Mill's liberal utilitarianism must make, broadly speaking, one of two kinds of arguments to preclude or mitigate this tension. One must argue that human nature is such that direct appeals to the standard of utility are suboptimal, or even self-defeating. *Only* by adopting a liberal system of rights can humans flourish, and so any tension that might arise between the demands of utility and the rights to freedom are only superficial and can be resolved within this framework of balancing competing interests. This is Mill's argument throughout, and Riley, among others concurs (Mill 1969c, p. 110; Riley 2007, p. 6). Another interpretive strategy is to argue that human nature may vary or be altogether different, but as society and human nature progress there will come a time when a liberal system of rights is the necessary condition for human flourishing. Gray argues that this theory of progress is implied in Mill's doctrine, and I agree that such an implication is at work in Mill's thought. These two arguments will be assessed in the last chapter.

Mill's life-long project was to deduce policies of moral political and social reform from the Principle of Utility: "actions are right in proportion as they tend to promote happiness, wrong as they tend to produce the reverse of happiness" (Mill 1969c, p. 210). The scope of his effort is enormous, as there is virtually no area of policy that he neglects to consider. At the same time, he was also concerned to reform individuals-only by actively developing one's character, or internal culture, could one experience the greatest amount of happiness. Mill's doctrine of reform can be summarized thusly:

> As the means of making the nearest approach to this ideal, utility would enjoin, first, that laws and social arrangements should place the happiness, or (as speaking practically it may be called) the interest, of every individual, as nearly as possible in harmony with the interest of the whole; and secondly, that education and opinion, which have so vast a power over human character, should so use that power as to establish in the mind of every individual an indissoluble association between his own happiness and the good of the whole; especially between his own happiness and the practice of such modes of conduct, negative and positive, as regard for the universal happiness prescribes: so that not only he may be unable to conceive the possibility of happiness to himself, consistently with conduct opposed to the general good, but also that a direct impulse to promote the general good may be in every individual one of the habitual

motives of action, and the sentiments connected therewith may fill a large and prominent place in every human being's sentient existence. (Mill 1969c, p. 218)

Because of the dual strategy of addressing institutions and individuals to achieve his utilitarian ideal, this presentation will begin by looking at how Mill understand the human mind to work, before moving on to discuss his moral principles and reform of political institutions.

Chapter 2 begins with an overview of Mill's experiential epistemology and then discusses the skeptical challenges it entails for his conceptions of self and matter. Next, the chapter looks at his psychological theory of associationism, to see how it accounts for mental phenomena that seem beyond his constrained epistemology. Once the general laws of associationism are made clear, it will then be possible to discuss how Mill endeavors to establish the new science of ethology, or character formation. Because character is one of the biggest determinants of behavior, and Mill's ideal of it is a central ingredient to happiness, he intended to inform all of his reforms with the principles of this new science. Ultimately, Mill fails to establish ethology, yet some of his writings can be considered as informal contributions to this science. *The Subject of Women* is a particularly good example of Mill's use of ethology, and so we will examine two such arguments he makes in the essay. Finally, the chapter presents the crucial distinction Mill makes between the logic of science, and the logic of art, or practice. Here, Mill lays the foundation for his entire liberal-utilitarian project, and so it is essential to understand how he envisions the ultimate standard of utility to justify subsidiary principles, such as the Principle of Liberty.

Mill never renounced his commitment to the standard of utility, and so Chapter 3 begins with an overview of the classical version of utilitarianism found in the thought of Jeremy Bentham. Second, the chapter looks at Mill's revisions to the standard, which in part intend to defend against some well-known criticism of Classical Utilitarianism. We also begin to see aspects of Mill's ideal character that he establishes as the end of his project of reform. Third, the chapter looks at Mill's much-maligned "proof" of utilitarianism, where again we see Mill's minimalist epistemology limiting the strengths of his claims. Like Mill's justification of inductive reasoning, we see Mill recasting logical argumentation as "naturalized" claims about empirical evidence for the truth of utilitarianism. Fourth, the chapter reviews the sanctions that enforce the utilitarian morality, and here we also see associationism playing a crucial role. If pleasure can come to be associated with almost any conduct, then there is the risk that Mill's moral psychology amounts to ethical relativism. Mill must therefore make the case for why the utilitarian ethic is superior to, or more natural than, others. Finally, the chapter reconstructs Mill's utilitarian conception of justice. The discussion of justice in *Utilitarianism* is the longest and most difficult of all the topics he addresses, and requires more interpretation. To a large extent, what Mill is attempting to do is to give customary morality a utilitarian foundation. His articulation is largely a formal one, leaving the content of morality to be detailed in *On Liberty*. Nonetheless, Mill attempts to tie together various arguments from psychology, sociology, anthropology in order to posit a conception of justice that is based on the promotion of general happiness, or expediency, but not equivalent to it.

The Principle of Liberty provides some of the content for Mill's moral theory, and so Chapter 4 begins with Mill's articulation of it, and then briefly discuss the first primary liberty Mill aims to protect, that of thought and discussion. Second, the chapter discusses the first challenge for applying the Principle of Liberty— the determination of whether an action affects other people without their consent. Third, the chapter makes the case that in addition to affecting other people, the action must also entail damage to certain, morally relevant interests in order for the action to be punishable. Fourth, the chapter discusses the second primary liberty Mill aims to protect, that of individuality. Individuality is the source of the most amount of pleasure, and so the fifth section of the chapter details the forms of influence individuals are liable to experience to help facilitate its development. Finally, chapter concludes by discussing a selection of Mill's applications of his Principle of Liberty, some of which clarify use, while others confuse it.

Despite criticizing Auguste Comte in a scathing essay, Mill nonetheless was deeply influenced by his positivism. Chapter 5 begins by discussing Mill's conception of history, which he conceives as unfolding and moving in stages. Second, the chapter looks as how this conception informs his theory of progress, that humanity is moving toward European values and institutions. Third, the chapter discusses Mill's presumption that for all developing civilizations, there will come a time when representative democracy is necessary for their continuing development. Representative democracy brings with it some unique challenges, and so the fourth section looks at the concepts of representation and interests. Another unique issue for democracy is the question of suffrage, and the fifth section of the chapter reviews some of Mill proposals for schemes of voting that reflect his formal and informal deference to the authority of expertise and knowledge. Finally, the chapter discusses how the totality of Mill's work can be summed up as constituting a new secular Religion of Humanity. "When a people internalize the utilitarian creed to such an extent that it governs every aspect of their being, it takes on religious qualities, despite being thoroughly secular." It is the point at which all utility costs of implementing Mill's principles will be outweighed by the maximal utility provided by this secular religion.

Because this exegesis of Mill's thought is primarily introductory, the book concludes by surveying some important criticisms of Mill's liberal utilitarianism. There is a large body of critical literature, but much of it are variations of the traditional critique. The last chapter will begin by reviewing Isaiah Berlin's seminal critique of Mill, which has spawned the revisionary attempt to meet Berlin's challenges. Berlin charges that Mill's argument in *On Liberty* is incoherent, and that he fails in his efforts to derive the values of liberty and individuality from the fundamental value of utility. Next, John Gray takes up this critique where Berlin leaves off, and ascribes to Mill a form of value pluralism that proves incompatible with his commitment to utilitarianism. Beyond the incoherency of Mill's liberal utilitarianism, Gray goes on to argue that Mill's project, like all Enlightenment ideologies that implicitly or explicitly rely on a theory of progress, are no longer empirically sustainable in light of recent historical developments. As I will show, some of Berlin and Gray's criticisms can be met, while the larger question as to the empirical sustainability of Mill's project remains, I believe, to be an open question.

CHAPTER TWO

Method and character

The most fundamental preliminaries of Mill's thought are laid bare for all to examine. His epistemology and scientific method help us understand his moral and political principles, but they also prove to be his doctrine's primary weakness. Throughout his writings, Mill promotes a particular ideal of character that is supposed to be the key to experiencing the most amount of happiness. However, the more he describes and romanticizes this ideal, the less it seems a product of inductive science, and more a projection of a particular conception of human flourishing. Though many of Mill's writings are now largely considered historical relics in the development of various fields of inquiry, they are essential to understanding his project of reform.

Experientialism

The study of knowledge, or epistemology, is often characterized as being a dichotomy between rationalists and empiricists, or more accurately as being between rationalist and empiricists ideas.[1] The two positions are not necessarily in opposition, as they can be used to account for different areas of knowledge, like scientific as opposed to moral knowledge. Rationalism posits that knowledge can only be generated by use of the human faculty of reason. Sensory information may inform reason, but reason alone is the source of knowledge. Descartes, Spinoza, and Leibniz are often cited as the paradigmatic examples of Continental rationalism

(Kenny 1985, p. 1). Arguably, the most famous rationalist in the Western tradition is Plato, who holds that everything in the physical world is nothing more than shadows of true forms or ideals. Empirical data derived from the senses are altogether inferior with regard to generating knowledge of the forms. Only the human capacity of reason could bring such ultimate knowledge. Plato's Parable of the Cave illustrates how sight can only provide a mere obfuscation of reality.

Mill comes from the British tradition of Empiricism, which includes Locke, Hume, and Bentham. The tradition can be said to extend as far back as to Hobbes, but Hobbes was also influential on some of the ideas of the rationalist, Leibniz. For Empiricists, the mind is a blank slate or *tabula rasa*, and all ideas are copies of sensory impressions. These simple ideas that reflect sensory impressions are then combined to form more complex ideas. For Mill, experience is the only source of direct information available to the mind, and so this extreme variant of empiricism is also characterized as experientialism, or phenomenalism.[2] "Truths are known to us in two ways: some are known directly, and of themselves; some through the medium of other truths" (Mill 1973, p. 6). Very little information could be known directly, or intuitively, and this limited foundation is a major influence on the character of his work in the philosophy of mind and moral philosophy. Conscious experience is one of the very few sources of truths that can be known directly. Beyond it, we can only infer other truths. This extremely limited foundation for knowledge faces several immediate challenges, all concerned with accepting the existence of information not immediately experienced. First of all, being limited only to sensory information, it is not clear how one could ever be certain of object permanence, or the existence of objects when they are not perceived by the senses. From a person's perspective, every time they close their eyes, the world disappears. This may seem a simplistic objection, but given the limited epistemology of Mill's empiricism, it is not clear how one could justifiably expect the world to persist when all sensory information is distorted, or ceases temporarily. It would appear to be beyond his empirical resources to have certainty that the world exists independently of perception. But in fact, Mill grants that the belief is justified, albeit in a qualified manner, provided that matter is understood to be the "Permanent Possibility of Sensation" (Mill 1979, p. 186). Because the human mind is capable of the expectation of sensation, individuals are justified in their belief in the permanence of reality. For having such a constrained epistemology, it is not surprising to find Mill hedging his conception of matter, lest he descend into a profound skepticism like that of Hume. Instead, he recasts matter as a *possibility*, which even a skeptic might accept, except for the fact of its *permanence*.

The second immediate challenge Mill faces as a phenomenalist is to establish the existence of other people and their minds. If the phenomenalist can only be certain about her own experiences, how can she accept that other people and their experiences are equally permanent and legitimate? Mill's rather pragmatic account is one of analogy. Other people have physical bodies that the phenomenalist can sense, and such bodies are similar to her own. She can therefore infer from the fact that other people report having experiences that collectively comprise a self, just like her *self*. Finally, other people behave in certain ways that seem to confirm the existence of their minds. But, by allowing the belief in other's mind, and one's own for that matter, Mill is not describing a "common theory of Mind, as a so-called Substance" (Mill 1979, p. 206). In other words, Mill is not positing metaphysical conception of the mind, or even anything beyond mere bundles of sensations. The self is not something that exists prior to experience. The self simply *is* experience. How Mill overcomes these two challenges can only be explained after discussing the central role of associationism below. However, one of the key unifying aspects of both matter and minds is memory, which is the third major challenge Mill must overcome.

The reliability of memory may seem initially like a nonissue for the phenomenalist, but the reality of past conscious experiences is as remote and uncertain as the existence of objects when one cannot sense them, or of other people's minds. It cannot be overemphasized how minimalist the phenomenalist's epistemological foundation is—*only* immediate, conscious sense experience can provide direct, reliable information, everything else must be inferred. That is to say, only the infinitely brief moment of experience is directly known before it is instantaneously relegated to memory, which is beyond experience. People generally take for granted that their memories are reliable, even though the certainty of such a belief is not always justified. Science has repeatedly demonstrated the unreliability of even the most vivid memories, such as with eyewitness testimony in court, and science fiction has explored the possibility of strategically implanting and removing memories.[3] In order to have any certainty in the coherency of the self, it will be necessary to establish the reliability of memory. Memory, in fact, is so foundational that along with conscious experience, Mill accepts it as the only *other* source of reliable information. No further experiential explanation can be given for the reliability of memory, beyond the fact that humans can (in general) rely on it. For a phenomenalist, this is quite a concession to the rationalists. Not surprisingly then, Mill's position on memory has attracted harsh criticism from both his contemporaries and our own. The attacks come from both sides of the epistemological divide. Some wonder why not expand the scope of direct knowledge to allow other essential aspects of the phenomenalist ontology, like matter.[4] Others argue that the fact that Mill cannot rely on experience to establish such a foundational aspect of his epistemology, subverts his entire experiential project (Ward 1860, pp. 5–6, 25–9).[5] Despite these continuing challenges, Mill's acceptance of experience and memory as being direct and intuitive remain a modest foundation upon which to build a theory of knowledge. Beyond these two sources of reliable knowledge, Mill must rely on other human faculties in order to accumulate new knowledge; in particular, people must use their capacity for reason.

When it comes to inferring from direct knowledge to new knowledge, Mill's methodology is as constrained as his foundation. Because conscious experience and memory are the only two justifiable sources of direct knowledge, Mill argues that the only way to generate new knowledge is by inductive reasoning, which he defines as "Generalization from Experience" (Mill 1973, p. 306). But for Mill, inductive reasoning is not so much about reasoning from the past to the future, than it is reasoning from the known to the unknown. On what grounds, it can rightly be asked, do we have to presume that the unknown will be like the known? Even though repeated observations may demonstrate that dropping an egg will result in its breaking, can we really be certain that the next time we drop an egg, it will break? Famously, Hume says absolutely not (Hume 1896, p. 270). For him, even though it is a habit of mind and painful to think otherwise, we have no logical reason to be certain in our conviction that the future will be like the past (or that the unknowns will be like the knowns, to use Mill's terminology) (Ibid.). Mill avoids this profound skepticism by presupposing a theory about nature, specifically that it is uniform.

We must first observe, that there is a principle implied in the very statement of what induction is; an assumption with regard to the course of nature and the order of the universe; namely, that there are such things in nature as parallel cases; that what happens once, will, under a sufficient degree of similarity of circumstances, happen again, and not only again, but as often as the same circumstances recur (Mill 1973, p. 306).

The uniformity of nature may well justify inductive reasoning, but it introduces a totally new question about nature. Mill is here referencing another fundamental debate surrounding the causal nature of the universe, determinism. Determinism is the idea that every action in nature, including human action, is causally determined by preceding conditions. These are two separate questions—is nature causally determined, and is induction valid? Mill answers in the affirmative to both questions. What evidence does Mill provide in support of the uniformity thesis of nature? The thesis is confirmed "in the actual course of nature", that is, every time we employ inductive reasoning (Ibid.). Unless Mill is willing to expand the scope of intuition to establish the reliability of induction, he seems trapped in the circular arguments of justifying the method of induction with the theory of uniformity, which in turn is supported by evidence established inductively. Consequently, despite the relative influential stature Mill attained, his "justification-in-practice" explanation was attacked first by T. H. Greene and the British Idealists of the late nineteenth century, who rejected empiricism altogether, and then later by Logical Positivists of the Vienna Circle who attempted to combine rationalism with empiricism (Skorupski 1998, p. 4). Despite its logical problems, many seem to recognize that Mill's conception of the self and his epistemology foreshadow the naturalized epistemology of W. V. O. Quine.[6] Up to the twentieth century, epistemologists concerned themselves in large part with responding to the problem of skepticism—the justification of knowledge. In an influential 1969 article entitled, "Epistemology Naturalized", Quine proposes recasting the debate over the justification of knowledge not as one of philosophy and logic, but as one of psychology. In other words, instead of exploring the philosophical justification individuals have for their knowledge, scholars should instead focus, *empirically*, on the processes by which individuals acquire and use knowledge, which is similar to how Mill employs his empiricism to address seemingly metaphysical theories like causality, and concepts like intuitive knowledge. For sure important differences remain, but anyone wanting to assess Mill's relevance today, or situate his thought historically, must acknowledge this commonality.

Associationism

The competing epistemological methodologies of rationalism and empiricism are best understood as *aspects* of larger doctrines, rather than as competing systems in their own right. Schools of thought that contain both aspects can still be at odds with each other. As described above, despite embracing the banner of empiricism, Mill accepts the reliability of memory, independent of experience, which precludes the profound skepticism of other empiricists, like Hume. Another school of thought, the Scottish Common Sense tradition, also employs elements of empiricism and rationalism. Conscious experience is the primary source of reliable information, but at the same time, individuals have innate dispositions to believe certain nonexperiential cognitive states, which also serve as intuitive knowledge. The best known exponent of this tradition is William Hamilton. His noteworthiness is less for the strength of his ideas, and more for the fact that Mill devotes an entire treatise to a devastating attack of his contribution to the Scottish Common Sense tradition.

For the Scottish Tradition, the central method for generating knowledge is introspection, the process of self-attending to one's conscious mind. Sensory information is a part of consciousness, but so too are the thoughts and feelings of the individual. For example, every act of perception entails simultaneous confirmation of the existence of both the self and reality. Hamilton calls this feature of the mind the Duality of Consciousness. Whereas for Mill, the establishment of an enduring self and an external world independent of perception are learned behaviors, for Hamilton the simple act of attending to an object confirms both ego and nonego (Mill 1979, p. 150). In fact, introspection produces lots of reliable information completely independent of experience because of the aforementioned innate dispositions that all people share. Mill rejects introspection. Although introspection could report the contents of the mind, it could not differentiate between innate ideas and learned ones. The only circumstances in which introspection could reveal the origins of our thoughts would be prior to the mind having any experiences at all, that is, just after birth.

> The proof that any of the alleged Universal Beliefs, or Principles of Common Sense, are affirmations of consciousness, supposes two things; that the beliefs exist, and that there are no means by which they could have been acquired. The first is in most cases undisputed, but the second is a subject of inquiry which often taxes the utmost resources of psychology. (Mill, 1979, p. 140)

Mill rejects introspection as a method of self-knowledge, because it merely accepts the contents of the mind at face value, and forgoes any deeper analysis. Crucially, it cannot differentiate between the learned ideas and mental states, and those which are innate and reflect human nature.

Describing the contents of the mind is part of Mill's "psychological method" but following Locke, the primary goal of psychology is to discover the *origins* of our ideas. This endeavor is more than simply isolating the preceding ideas and states of mind; it is also discovering the laws that govern their succession. Mill's psychological method examines the complex ideas of mental states and breaks them down into constituent and antecedent parts (Wilson 1990, p. 111). Constituent parts are present in the complex idea whereas antecedent parts may have a causal relationship with the complex idea or mental state. Such a technique is only possible because the general laws of psychology have been obtained already, using the "ordinary methods of experimental inquiry." The psychological method entails applying these general laws to "actual phenomenon" to see how far they can account for them (Mill 1974, p. 853).

Mill provides no systematic account of the general laws that govern the mental phenomena, but between several writings it is possible to construct an overview of his science of mind. Starting with notes that Mill adds to his father's *Analysis of the Phenomenon of Human Mind*, the younger Mill situates himself squarely in the tradition of associationism, one of the dominant theories of mind that include Hume, Locke, Hobbes, and Aristotle (Garforth 1979, p. 47). Psychology, according to the younger Mill, being concerned with thoughts, emotions, volitions, and sensations was not an experimental science yet, so Mill's contribution was to clarify and systematize the empirical theories of his inherited associationism

(Wilson 1990, chapter 4). The science was in its nascent stages when Mill was writing, and so his goal was primarily to establish its explanatory limits. In *A System of Logic*, Mill lays out how the same methodological principles of the natural sciences can be brought to bear on the "moral sciences," or those pertaining to the human mind and behavior. In *An Examination of Alexander Hamilton's Philosophy*, Mill begins the process of using the general principles of associationism to account for mental phenomena that were until then thought to be intuitive. Mill's entire conception of psychology, including his psychological method described above, is premised on the validity of laws of associationism, which he takes for granted. The general laws of associationism, like the most general laws of physics with regard to the physical world, describe the macro behavior of the mind. Mill is attempting to deduce from those laws, as many corollaries as possible to explain specific mental phenomena and individual behavior.

Mill's associationist psychology is concerned with states of the mind. As an experientialist, the primary data for Mill's science are sensations in the nervous system and their corresponding ideas in the mind. When an idea is generated directly by the nervous system in this way, the interaction is governed by the laws of physiology. When an idea causes another idea in the mind, the succession is not governed by physiology, but by the laws of psychology. As a fledging science, Mill was attempting to justify the independence of the general laws of psychology as distinct from those of physiology, another science in its infancy. During Mill's time, some thinkers hypothesized that beyond the nervous system, some ideas of the mind were localized in certain parts of the brain, and that the movement from one idea to another was actually one part of the brain interacting with another, and that the seemingly independent laws of the mind were really derivative of the laws of the body. Auguste Comte, a contemporary and important influence on Mill's thought, nonetheless broke with Mill on the status psychology. Comte thought psychology a pseudoscience, on par with astrology, and preferred phrenology as the proper study of the mind.[7] Interestingly, it is now widely understood that some mental phenomena are localized in specific parts of the brain, such as consciousness residing primarily in the frontal cortex, and yet psychology persists as an independent science. Mill understood, presciently, that physiology would occupy a larger role in the understanding of mental phenomena once it matured as a science. And if we expand Mill's conception of physiology to include the growing field of neuroscience, he was surely correct. Nonetheless, because of the observable "uniformities" with which mental states do appear to follow each other under certain conditions, the science of psychology, as distinct from physiology, is a valuable approach to understanding the mind.

The most general law of psychology underpins Mill's experientialist epistemology and had been acknowledged as long back as Hobbes. The external world "presses" on the nervous system, in the form of touch, smell, taste, feeling, and sight, which then converts that stimuli into a corresponding idea. Once an idea has been created in the mind, it can then be recalled and "experienced" to a lesser degree without the original stimulation. Using memory, which Mill accepts as a source of direct knowledge, one can experience the sight of a beautiful sunset, or the smell and taste of a delicious meal entirely within one's mind. The same applies to imagination. Mill states that an artist who conjures up a mental picture in the mind of an image, or setting, can store the idea in the mind and recall it without repeating the original and spontaneous process of artistic creation. Such experiences and memories are often connected to powerful emotions, which like sensations, can also be recalled and experienced in like manner (Mill 1974, p. 852). Mill calls this justifiable reliance on memory, "expectation" (Mill 1979, p. 177). Once an idea exists in the mind, the laws of associationism govern its' interactions. The first law states that similar ideas tend to excite each other. The second law states that when two sensory impressions have been experienced together, either simultaneously or in quick succession, they tend to become associated. In other words, once two impressions are associated, stimulating or recalling one impression will result in experiencing the other. The third law states that the intensity of the impressions, as well as the frequency of the pairings, will strengthen the association equally (Mill 1974, p. 852). The fourth law states that when two or more ideas become strongly associated, they can become inseparable in the mind (Mill 1979, p. 177). When ideas combine to form new ideas in the mind, they can associate mechanically, or chemically. When two ideas associate mechanically, the antecedent ideas are present in the complex new idea. Mill describes how the complex idea of an orange consists of a round object that tastes citrus-y, and is a color that is between red and yellow: These different sensations that associate together are designated as the fruit, orange. Sometimes, only one of these sensations is necessary to conjure up in the mind the complex whole, such as the taste of citrus alone. This particular sensation is constituent of the idea of an orange, and easily identifiable if one deconstructs the orange. Other complex ideas are produced by chemical association, meaning that the antecedent ideas that associate are no longer present in the resultant complex idea. The complex idea is greater than the sum of its parts and so is *generated* by the antecedent parts, rather than consist of them (Mill 1974, p. 854). For Mill, these laws explain how much of the knowledge taken to be intuitive, is really the product of experience and associationism. Two examples of complex ideas that associate chemically, and so no longer contain their antecedent parts are matter and the self.

Hamilton argues that humans intuitively know and understand the existence of matter and the self. Against this quasi-rationalist claim, Mill argues that the idea of matter, independent of human perception, is actually a complex association of several simpler sensations and their corresponding ideas. Once a person has some experience of the world, they can then store that experience in memory and recall it at any time. One may only be experiencing a very small and isolated set of sensations generated by their immediate surroundings, but they are also capable of expecting a vast number of other possible experiences in other circumstances. These other possible sensations are organized according to the laws of association, and so many will be inseparable from each other. As the store of possible sensations grows and becomes further associated with newer and repeated experiences, it takes on the unique characteristic of forming a background set of expectations while one actually experiences some aspect of it. One's conscious experience of some matter may temporarily cease, but the possibilities remain, independent of our will and hence take on a *permanent* quality (Mill 1979, p. 182). Similarly, the concept of the self is also the product of antecedent ideas, and can be regarded as a permanent possibility for the same reasons that matter takes on this quality. All conscious experiences are accompanied by the background of memories of previous experiences, as well as expectations of future ones. The unifying thread of this series of ideas, and that which enables the conception of the self, is simply the *belief* that one really did have the experiences stored in memory, and that one will experience the expected sensations. This is as far as Mill can go with his experiential account of the self. As he readily admits, if we want to conceive of the self as a series of sensations, then it paradoxically must be a series of sensations which is somehow aware of itself. To put the paradox more succinctly, a sense organ cannot sense itself, and so a series of sensations cannot be of themselves. The alternative explanation is that there is at the core of the self, something that transcends experience, such as an essence or a soul, which of course, is beyond resources of experientialism and empiricism. Hence, Mill concludes his account of the self in a somewhat cautious manner: "by far the wisest thing we can do, is to accept the inexplicable fact, without any theory of how it takes place; and when we are obliged to speak of it in terms which assume a theory, to use them with a reservation as to their meaning" (Mill 1979, p. 194).

As an outspoken reformer of law, culture, education, and even family relations, the central role of Mill's associationist psychology cannot be understated. In order to argue how the world should be, it is first necessary to understand how the world is. Even though associationist psychology is now largely considered a simplistic and antiquated account of the human mind, it is the underlying framework upon which Mill makes his normative claims about the world. Associationism plays an especially crucial role in his account of the utilitarian morality. It serves two functions, one critical, the other positive. The chief object of criticism in *Utilitarianism* is the idea that morality is known through intuition and reason. Intuitionists argue that morality is known through reason, and its authority is similarly self-evident, or a priori. Apart from being unsystematic, ambiguous, and inherently conservative, the novelty of Mill's argument is to show that such doctrines implicitly rely on the empirical consequences of their ethical principles, especially on one's *happiness*, for their widespread adoption. Even the famous first principle of Immanuel Kant, preeminent of all rationalists according to Mill, that one should only obey "the rule on which thou actest would admit of being adopted as a law by all rational beings," is only practical by appealing to experience (Immanuel Kant quoted in Mill 1969c, p. 207). As Mill correctly points out, there is nothing in the principle that necessarily precludes immoral behavior, apart from the undesirable consequences of such behavior being universally adopted. In other words, morality cannot be established by reason alone, it is learned from experience. By associating various external sanctions, in particular pain and pleasure, with ethical rules, one develops a moral conscience that guides behavior. Like other ideas thought to originate in intuition, Mill argues that morality is acquired by experience and association. His purpose in *Utilitarianism* is to argue that only ethical rules that can be shown to promote happiness should be adopted. In fact, all of Mill's moral and social reforms should be considered part of a larger project of getting people to associate their own happiness with the happiness of those around them and eventually all of humanity.

The second crucial role that associationism plays in Mill's account of morality is to explain the inherent value of virtue. One of the challenges for Mill is to respond to the criticism that the utilitarian conception of human nature is one of mere selfishness or psychological egoism. Lord Macualay, for example, in his essay, "Mill, on Government", attacks the Classical Utilitarianism of Bentham and James Mill for its failure to justify any theory of government or morality from the premise that humans do not pursue anything other than their own self-interest or happiness (Macaulay 1860). The Classical Utilitarians relied on the argument that individuals are capable of reasoning that it is in their own long-term interests to adhere to norms of justice and morality. The critics argue that only with an independent moral sentiment at work in the mind could the more selfish and shortsighted desires of Man be restrained. Mill recognized the strength of this critique, and so attempts to reconcile the fundamental desire for pleasure that underpins the utilitarian conception of human nature, with the authentic desire for virtue, independent of the pleasure it may produce. (Wilson 1990, chapter 4). His mentors were more concerned with deterring criminal acts, whereas Mill understood the importance of preventing criminal desires. At the same time, Mill was attempting to deduce law and policy from general principles, which were ultimately deduced from one first principle. Mill thusly begins *Utilitarianism* with a firm commitment to the utilitarian premise of human motivation, "pleasure, and freedom from pain, are the only things desirable as ends; and all desirable things (which are as numerous in the utilitarian as in any other scheme) are desirable either for their pleasure inherent in themselves, or as means to the promotion of pleasure and the prevention of pain" (Mill 1969c, p. 210). This "Theory of Life", stated early on in the essay, would seem to suggest that when people behave virtuously, it is only as a means to pleasure, which would not be virtuous at all, but merely self-interested. However, the Theory of Life operates at a fundamental level of psychology. Through experience, the desire for pleasure becomes associated with all sorts of actions, some mechanically, and some chemically. Virtuous behavior may have originally been only a means to pleasure, but as pleasure is repeatedly experienced through this particular vehicle, pleasure becomes chemically associated with the virtuous behavior. Pleasure may have been an antecedent sensation, along with the virtuous behavior, but through the repeated pairings, virtue becomes desired for itself, as the sensation of pleasure is no longer present in the newly formed desire for virtuous behavior. In fact, many of the ingredients of happiness come to be acquired in this way. Some elements of happiness are consciously desired as inherently pleasurable, such as fine food and wine; yet others, such as physical exertion or intellectual engagement are desired for themselves because of a deep-seated and obscured association to pleasure. Individuals may be born with nothing other than hedonistic desires, but Mill's mental crisis taught him that the paradoxical nature of happiness is that one could not attain it if one directly aimed for it. Happiness is only possible by pursuing activities for themselves, and then enjoying the pleasure associated with it. As he puts it, "Ask yourself whether you are happy, and you cease to be so" (Mill 1981, p. 147). Mill's associationism provides the resources for his life-long project to refashion society so that individuals are socialized to connect only utility-maximizing desires with their happiness. Such a grand endeavor would only be possible with an understanding of the general laws of mind. And yet despite Mill's employment of associationism to explain many phenomena of the mind, there remains a central tension between his science and the goal of reform to which he applies it.

As described above, one of the foundational generalizations that all people make from the experience of the world is the uniformity of nature, or the idea that the world is causally determined. As one repeatedly observes that certain circumstances in nature always result in some certain event, one comes to realize that every action in nature is causally determined by preceding conditions. Such uniformity is what enables our scientific understanding of the world, and-Mill was convinced-also enables our understanding of the workings of the human mind. The problem is, if the mind and behavior are causally determined to such an extent that general laws of behavior can be induced, how can anyone claim to possess free will? This is a proverbial and potentially crippling problem for Mill, as well as for other philosophers. Without free will, how can society hold anyone morally responsible for their behavior if they had no choice but to behave in that way? The concept of responsibility itself is premised on the existence of free will. Moreover, if one wants to reform individual behavior as Mill does, how can anyone's behavior be altered from the causal chain of events that stretches back to the very origins of the species? Mill was well aware of this problem, and he addresses it in *A System of Logic.*

Mill casts the debate as being between those who consider human behavior to be causally determined, and espouse the doctrine of Philosophical Necessity, and those who think that decision-making transcends physical experiences and appeal to a metaphysical theory of free will. The doctrine of Necessity is "that, given the motives that are present to an individual's mind, and given likewise the character and disposition of the individual, the manner in which he will act could be unerringly inferred: that if we knew the person thoroughly, and knew all the inducements which are acting upon him, we could foretell his conduct with as much certainty as we can predict any physical event" (Mill 1974, p. 837).

Mill thinks there is sufficient evidence for this doctrine, as it is supported by everyday experiences with people. In fact, among close friends and relatives, it might even be offensive if one failed to anticipate another's behavior in commonplace circumstances. But the object of Mill's criticism is not those who hold the metaphysical theory of free will. Mill rejects that humans have a decision-making capacity that is free of any causal relations in the physical world. But even though Mill rejects this metaphysical position, in practice he sees it as being closer to the truth than the position of hard-line determinists, like the Utopian, Robert Owen. It is against *this* camp that Mill attempts to clarify his position on the question of free will. Owen and his followers rejected the concept of responsibility, as they considered all human action to be the product of circumstance and character, and character was made for individuals by others. Mill agrees that behavior is determined by character and circumstances, and that character is in large part a product of education and upbringing. Where Mill parts with the Owenites is that Mill thinks one can influence the development of one's own character, if one so chooses. And whereas the Owenites would claim that the desire to alter one's character is itself beyond one's control, Mill claims that the desire can come from experience, either of the painful consequences of one's current character, or the feeling of admiration for another's character (Mill 1974, p. 841). Mill claims that the Owenites wrongly take the term "necessary" to mean "inevitable." For Mill, the term "necessary" conveys the fact that for the causal chain of events leading to some action A, unless some new causal antecedent intervenes, action A will happen. It is less about the *ability* to alter one's character than about the emergence of the *desire* to do so, which will happen given certain experiences. But again, what Mill takes for granted—the ability to alter one's character—the Owenites can claim is beyond the control of those who are denied certain experiences. Hence, Mill's argument with the Owenites reaches an impasse: either Mill and the Owenites infinitely regress down the path of Mill positing the ability to influence one's character and hence behavior, and the Owenites questioning this ability's origins; or Mill concedes that there will be some individuals who, for reasons *beyond* their control, never develop the ability to alter their characters, and are therefore compelled to act a certain way. Mill never concedes the impasse, but in several writings, such as *On Liberty* and the *Subjection of Women*, Mill's premise is that for large numbers of people deeply influenced by custom and conventional social norms, the ability to alter one's character has been suppressed. Short of widespread reform of cultural and social institutions, such people are confined to their suboptimal characters.

Character

The goal of reforming society in order to maximize aggregate happiness is only possible because of an understanding of the fundamental causal laws of the mind: individuals desire their own pleasure and happiness. From experience, pleasure can come to be associated with various activities to such a degree that the activities are then desired for themselves. Mill does not think that pleasure is wholly subjective, and beyond the criticism of others. One of the changes Mill makes to the Classical Utilitarianism of Bentham and his father is to argue that there is an important distinction between lower and higher pleasures. The higher pleasures are not simply activities that yield more pleasure, rather they are activities that produce a categorically *superior* kind of pleasure (Mill 1969c, p. 212). Despite the introduction of this hierarchy possibly violating Mill's Theory of Life (specifically, what is it, other than pleasure, that makes the higher pleasures inherently more desirable? see Chapter 3), it is necessary for Mill's efforts to move the utilitarian conception of happiness from the Epicureans' passive mental state to Aristotle and the Romantic's active human flourishing. Reform, therefore, entails first altering cultural norms and social institutions so that only utility-maximizing behaviors and pursuits get associated with one's own pleasure, and second facilitating the development of desires for higher pleasures, even though Mill recognized that this development may entail some "discontent" (Mill 1969c, p. 211). Fully enjoying poetry, for example, will entail developing an appreciation for language and rhythm that may not be pleasurable to the uninitiated. Such sweeping reform would not be possible by merely endeavoring to alter people's behavior. In order to dislodge the dominant social norms preventing people from flourishing, Mill must change people's *normative attitudes* about their behavior as well. Hence, in *Utilitarianism*, Mill states that the goal of his reform is the general cultivation of nobleness of character (Mill 1969c, p. 214). One's character is the key to maximizing individual and general happiness because it is the primary determinant of behavior. But character is not the sum total of behavior, because "A person whose desires and impulses are his own – are the expression of his own nature, as it has been developed and modified by his own culture – is said to have character" (Mill 1977b, p. 264). Behavior is the best evidence for character, but it is more the *reasons* why one behaves in a certain way that demonstrates one's character. If one's desires merely reflect the internalization of prevailing social norms, then the desires are not an expression of one's character. But if one has reflected on one's desires and has willfully chosen to accept prevailing social norms, then such behavior can be considered a reflection of one's character.

In part because of Mill's own peculiar upbringing, many of his published writings can be considered contributions to the study of character. In order to facilitate "nobleness of character," Mill proposes a new science, which he calls ethology.

Human beings do not all feel and act alike in the same circum-stances; but it is possible to determine what makes one person, in a given position, feel or act in one way, another in another; how any given mode of feeling and conduct, compatible with the general laws (physical and mental) of human nature, has been, or may be, formed. In other words, mankind have not one universal character, but there exist universal laws of the Formation of Character . . . it is on these that every rational attempt to construct the science of human nature in the concrete, and for practical purposes, must proceed. (Mill 1974, p. 864)

The general laws of psychology alone would not suffice because they say nothing of how the particulars of one's circumstance interact with the unique desires and dispositions of the mind. In *A System of Logic*, where Mill establishes his inductive methodology and epistemology, he carefully situates ethology between the general laws of psychology and "Empirical Law," which are limited and superficial observations of regularity in nature[8] (Mill 1974, p. 861). Empirical laws are only valid once they are shown to be applications of general laws. This connection is only possible with the existence of axiomata media, or middle principles, connecting the empirical laws to the ultimate general laws. For example, an empirical law might be that the leaves of trees turn from green to gold before falling off every Autumn. Knowing the general laws of thermodynamics will not go very far to explain this behavior of trees. Only with an understanding of the middle principles of photosynthesis can we see the general laws of thermodynamics at work in the changing colors of leaves. Mill gives the example of behavior displayed by youth and the aged. It is an empirical law that young people tend to act recklessly; and the aged tend to act more cautiously. The general laws of psychology cannot explain these character traits without the ethological principle that repeated misfortunes and encounters with the many dangers in life will lead to a cautious and more thoughtful character. Once this principle has been deduced, we can see that it is not age itself which tempers inclination but repeated experiences of the adversities of life (Mill 1974, p. 862). Mill concedes that even after fully mapping out the laws that govern character formation, in practice one could never know all of the details of any given circumstance to fully predict what character trait will be produced. However, one could know enough about a circumstance and apply ethological theory to determine what sort of character trait *tends* to be produced in that circumstance. This level of certainty is a limit to the power of ethology, but would suffice to rearrange social institutions to facilitate certain character traits and hinder others (Mill 1974, p. 870).

There are several possible methodologies for establishing ethological principles, most of which are unfeasible. Controlled experimentation, a common and very powerful tool in psychology, would be inappropriate, in part because of the totalitarian control over a person's life that would be required. The experimenter would need to rear a child from birth and control every aspect of their existence in order to determine how circumstance affected the emergence of some trait. Moreover, even if an experimenter had such an unfortunate subject, it would be impossible to control the subject's circumstances to such a degree as to eliminate any possible confounding variable. A further point that Mill does not consider, and one for which his own life is illustrative, is that the subject of the ethologist's experiments would have such an inhuman existence that it would be impossible to generalize the results to the rest of the population. The second methodology that Mill dismisses is observation, by which Mill refers to the correlational study. First, the process of ascertaining someone's character to establish a baseline is inherently contentious—different people who know some person well may still disagree as to the description of her character. Second, character traits are only revealed over time; any single or few observations would constitute weak evidence of a particular trait. Finally, the same difficulties in controlling the circumstantial variables within an experiment are multiplied when outside of the laboratory. It would be impossible to isolate which aspect of the environment is correlating with which aspect of the subject's character. All one could accomplish with observation is to make the superficial generalizations about types of characters correlating with types of circumstances. Causality would be impossible to ascertain, and such observations would only have the status of empirical laws. However, such observation does form a *part* of the methodology of ethology. Ethology is primarily a deductive science. Ethological theories about the influences of particular circumstances must be deduced from the general laws of psychology and then verified empirically. It is therefore crucial for the ethologist to simultaneously observe different people, and to amass as many empirical laws as possible to test the ethological theories (Mill 1974, p. 873).

Unfortunately, the methodological groundwork was as far as Mill came to establishing the science of ethology. Nonetheless, both before and after *A System of Logic*, Mill stresses the necessity of understanding the principles of character formation to any scientific study of society.[9] Many of his most widely read essays are implicit applications of the middle principles of ethology. In Particular, *Considerations of Representative Government* and *On Liberty*, the chief reasons for his principles are their effect on character development (see Chapters 5 and 4, respectively). Mill does not present the principles as being part of the science of ethology, but with an understanding the general laws of psychology outlined above, we can see how they are. However, one of the best applications of ethology in Mills writings comes in the *Subjection of Women*. In the essay, Mill not only gives an ethological account of what he takes to be the female character *en masse*, he also discusses the ethological conditions for instilling in children the moral character necessary for increasing the stock of general happiness.

Ethology in The Subjection of Women

Along with Mary Wollstonecraft in the eighteenth century, Mill is often cited as one of the first philosophers to argue for equality between men and women. As with *On Liberty*, in *The Subjection of Women*, Mill is as interested in overturning social and cultural norms, as he is in changing law. Well aware of the controversial nature of his conclusions, Mill strategically deploys several different arguments to make the case that women should possess the same property rights, employment opportunities, and suffrage that men possess. Two such arguments are: first, to critically account for the current state of subjection that women are in, specifically to debunk the claim that the current social inequalities are natural; and second, to describe several key benefits to society, once legal and cultural equality is recognized between men and women. Both of these arguments illustrate the use of ethology to achieve Mill's larger goals of reform.

One of the main obstacles to reforming the treatment of women in society is the powerful idea that the inferior status of women is natural. Mill attributes this idea to Aristotle, but goes on to describe how generally, all individuals and groups who exercise tyrannical power over others think that the relationship is natural. Moreover, the subjection of women seems almost universal, in both time and across cultures. But despite some examples of powerful woman in history, no less than the Queen of England, Mill points out that when people say that it is natural for woman to be subordinated to men, what they really mean is that it is *customary* (Mill 1984a, p. 270). To claim that the subjection of women, or of any people, is natural, is to imply that there is something about their psychological and genetic makeup, or characters, that renders their subordination appropriate, and possibly even better for *them*. To claim that the subjection is customary is merely to state that no other relationship between men and women has yet existed, which Mill readily admits (some historical and contemporary exceptions aside). The latter claim is a much more modest one, but Mill argues that it is the only one justified by evidence, or rather, the lack of evidence.

> I deny that any one knows, or can know, the nature of the two sexes, as long as they have only been seen in their present relation to one another. If men had ever been found in society without women, or women without men, or if there had been a society of men and women in which the women were not under the control of the men, something might have been positively known about the mental and moral differences which may be inherent in the nature of each. (Mill 1984a, p. 276)

The natures of men and women are all-important facts, because many of the normative prescriptions about how to arrange society's institutions and laws turn on these fundamental data. The problem is that as long as the sexes exist in their current relationship of inequality, it is impossible to know their true natures, and that this fact is sufficient to justify a discussion of the prevailing norms that underpin the subjection of women.

The Subjection of Women was published 26 years after Mill's call for a new science of ethology in *A System of Logic*. Even though that call went largely unfulfilled, and Mill laments this fact in *Subjection*, its methods and purpose clearly underpin the main arguments for equality (Mill 1984a, p. 277). Women, as a group, clearly display some common behavior, such as their willingness to submit to men, and their lack of any ambition beyond the home, which would seem to support those who claim the subjection of women to be natural. But without fully accounting for their character it is impossible to know what aspects are an expression of their female nature, and what aspects have been socialized by a patriarchal society. For example, the law renders women thoroughly dependent on husbands, and grants husbands unqualified power over wives. Therefore, attracting good suitors is the most rational course of action for women. But there is a twist:

> All women are brought up from the very earliest years in the belief that their ideal of character is the very opposite to that of men: not self-will, and government by self-control, but submission, and yielding to the control of others. All the moralities tell them that it is the duty of women, and all the current sentimentalities that it is their nature, to live for others: to make complete abnegation of themselves, and to have no life but in their affections. (Mill 1984a, p. 271)

Mill, of course, recognized that men and women are naturally attracted to each other. But the subtle and powerful leverage that men possess over women in this regard is that women are socialized to believe that "meekness" and "submissiveness" are essential to their attractiveness (Mill 1984a, p. 272). Mill points out that men do not simply want women's obedience, they also want their sentiments, and so it is the *willingness* to submit that attracts men, not simply the submission. Once women begin families, their primary duties are as wife and mother, and so their ambitions are accordingly confined. Men are socialized to seek fame and success in life, whereas it would be "unfeminine" for women to do so outside of the home.

> The natural desire of consideration from our fellow creatures is as strong in a woman as in a man; but society has so ordered things that public consideration is in all ordinary cases, only attainable by her through the consideration of her husband or of her male relations, while her private consideration is forfeited by making herself individually prominent, or appearing in any other character than that of an appendage to men. (Mill 1984a, p. 320)

With all professional opportunities closed to women, and public opinion generally against women striving for notoriety, it is little wonder they limit their efforts to the home, and only enjoy the fame garnered by their husbands. But again, we see Mill claiming that this seemingly universal trait of women, is nothing more than the product of learning, and so not at all an expression of their true natures. In fact, "What is now called the nature of women is an eminently artificial thing - the result of forced repression in some directions, unnatural stimulation in others" (Mill 1984a, p. 271). Mill's ethological account of these two aspects of women's character is important because it subverts the powerful argument that the subjection is natural. However at the same time, it reveals the limits of ethology because even if the science was fully developed, it could not discover the true nature of women without isolating them from men. The true natures of men and women remain matters of speculation.[10]

Another important strand of Mill's argument for gender equality is the many advantages to society, like doubling the available workforce and intellectual capacity. In particular, Mill stresses that the greatest benefit to society would be the vast amount of gain to human nature that would result from equality between the men and women (Mill 1984a, p. 324). In fact, Mill claims that many vices so prevalent among humans, like selfishness, are learned traits that are perpetuated by the dominion that men have over women: "The self-worship of a monarch, or of a feudal superior, is matched by the self-worship of the male". People who acquire authority by birth display nothing but the "worst kind of pride," derived from the unjustified obedience of others. And when children grow up exposed to a general sense of superiority combined with a specific one, such as with a father over a mother, it amounts to a "regularly constituted Academy or Gymnasium for training them in arrogance and overbearingness" (Mill 1984a, p. 325). Regardless of any natural difference that may or may not exist between the sexes, from birth, boys are confronted with the incongruous power structure of the subordination of their mothers, combined with obedience to them.

> Think what it is to a boy, to grow up to manhood in the belief that without any merit or any exertion of his own . . . by the mere fact of being born a male he is by right the superior of all and every one of an entire half of the human race: including probably some whose real superiority to himself he has daily or hourly occasion to feel; but even If in his whole conduct he habitually follows a woman's guidance, still, if he is a fool, he thinks that of

course she is not, and cannot be, equal in ability and judgment to himself; and if he is not a fool, he does worse- he sees that she is superior to him, and believes that, notwithstanding her superiority, he is entitled to command and she is bound to obey. What must be the effect on his character, of this lesson? (Mill 1984a, p. 324)

The influence on the young boys' character is to subvert the grounds for a relationship of equality with women—the love and deference that they have for their mothers—with the hierarchy between men and women, modeled after their parents. This superiority that boys are taught transcends any respect they may have for women, and any evidence of women's comparable abilities. In light of the methodological limitations of ethology discussed above, it is impossible to say whether this is a *corruption* of human nature. Nonetheless, Mill argues that it is possible to change the influences on the formation of children's characters to facilitate not just a sense of equality between men and women but all morality.

The equality of married persons before the law, is not only the sole mode in which that particular relation can be made consistent with justice to both sides, and conducive to the happiness of both, but it is the only means of rendering the daily life of mankind, in any high sense, a school of moral cultivation. Though the truth may not be felt or generally acknowledged for generations to come, the only school of genuine moral sentiment is society between equals. (Mill 1984a, p. 293)

Because of the unique relationship that parents have with their children, the family is the earliest and the most formative influence on character-formation. Not only do parents explicitly instill morality in their children, but their relationship also forms a template upon which the children model their own dealings with the opposite sex. Society, with all its institutional and cultural influences, reinforces the lessons taught by the parents, and for Mill, the whole of human progress depends on there being equality in the family (Mill 1984a, p. 295).

The fundamental reform of English society being the goal, we can now see how crucial it was to focus on character-formation.

Laws could be changed by Parliament, but essays such as the *Subjection of Women, On Liberty,* and many others illustrate that the scope of Mill's efforts required a much broader and pervasive form of influence. Mill never established the new theoretical science of ethology to achieve these ends, and so many of his arguments were directed at one of its practical applications, education. Mill criticizes and comments on the administration of education, but in no writing gives a systematic account of a pedagogical method. Perhaps this is to be expected, because as Mill makes clear in his Inaugural Address to St Andrews University, he holds the broadest possible conception of education:

> Education, moreover, is one of the subjects which most essentially require to be considered by various minds, and from a variety of points of view. For, of all many-sided subjects, it is the one which has the greatest number of sides. Not only does it include whatever we do for ourselves, and whatever is done for us by others, for the express purpose of bringing us somewhat nearer to the perfection of our nature; it does more: in its largest acceptation, it comprehends even the indirect effects produced on character and on the human faculties, by things of which the direct purposes are quite different, by laws, by forms of government, by the industrial arts, by modes of social life; nay even by physical facts not dependent on human will; by climate, soil, and local position. Whatever helps to shape the human being, to make the individual what he is, or hinder him from being what he is not— is part of his education. (Mill 1984b, p. 217)

Thus conceived, the principles derived from the science of ethology would contribute to the field of education, but not define it. Education is much broader than the systematic influence of character. It includes the much narrower field of pedagogy, as well as any experience one might have that leaves a significant impression. Perhaps no such account could be given, but as has been detailed in an important contribution to Millian scholarship by F. W. Garforth, pedagogical aspects of Mill's theory of education can be identified as consequences of Mill's principles in various writings (Garforth 1979). For example, Mill's arguments for participatory democracy suggest that education should be an *active* process, giving enough information and guidance to students to have as much discretion in their studies as is practical. One of the arguments for freedom of speech is that only by defending our beliefs and opinions from opposing ones do we come to a full understanding of them. Students would therefore be expected to evaluate the strengths and weaknesses of different arguments, as well as be able to rigorously defend their own opinions. Finally, students would be immersed in classical and contemporary literature, as the appreciation of art utilizes certain capacities of the mind that are associated with a higher quality of pleasure than more pedestrian diversions. This last example illustrates a potential flaw in Mill's method. Using principles from psychology, ethology, and all of the "moral sciences", Mill's reform efforts have all focused on developing a particular type of character ideal that supposedly yields the most happiness. However, this method informs his arguments about *how* to achieve that ideal; they have no bearing on the determination of *what* that ideal is. As will be discussed in Chapter 6, one of the central problems for Mill is that the character ideal he promotes in his writings seems less like an empirically grounded conception of human nature and more like the projection of a parochial and Victorian conception of human flourishing.

The art of life

Before concluding our survey of Mill's scientific methods, it is important to note the ultimate limit to its authority. Mill was writing during a time when there did not exist rigid distinctions between the methodological and disciplinary modes of thinking and investigating that characterize the professional pursuit of knowledge today. As a social reformer, his arguments invoked and blended disparate claims that today would be considered epistemological, logical, psychological, and sociological. Science, in all its manifold departments, is a tool; it tells us only how nature works and expresses itself in empirical statements. But the project of reform is bigger than science, because reform entails the identification of goals toward which science works. Science only has instrumental value, because it has nothing to say about which goals are desirable. A very different mode of thinking is employed to make this fundamental determination. At the end of

A System of Logic, Mill makes a crucial distinction between the logic of science and the logic of Practice, or Art, which establishes the utilitarian framework for all of his moral, social, and political prescriptions.

A System of Logic is Mill's definitive account of logic and science, with special focus on the moral sciences of human nature. But science is a portion of the larger activity of Practice or Art, which has its own logic (I will henceforth only refer to Art). As Mill describes, the builder's art (construction) has as its first principle that buildings are good, or the medicinal art (medicine) that health is good. These first principles establish the ends toward which the logic of their practices are directed. Once the end of the Art is established, different sciences are brought together to determine the best techniques to achieve that end. The specific technologies and methods of construction have become more efficient and precise over the centuries, as advances in material sciences and engineering have proceeded generally, leading to better buildings overall. Similarly, as diagnostic, surgical, and pharmaceutical techniques improve, as well as our understanding of the human body grows, medicine makes huge strides in promoting health. These sciences are essential to their respective Art, but they are entirely subservient to their ends:

> The art proposes to itself an end to be attained, defines the end, and hands it over to the science. The science receives it, considers it as a phenomenon or effect to be studied, and having investigated its causes and conditions, sends it back to art with a theorem of the combinations of circumstances, and according as any of them are or are not in human power, pronounces the end attainable or not. (Mill 1974, p. 944)

Science merely sets out the best theoretical strategies to attain the end, only Art can formally sanction a strategy and make it a precept or rule. The practices of Art are changing indefinitely, for the rules and precepts of the Art are based on scientific knowledge and so will evolve as the corresponding sciences evolve. As Mill puts it, Science speaks in the indicative mood, asserting statements of fact; whereas Art speaks in the imperative mood, conferring value to its subservient practices. The only evaluative standard within the

Art, is conduciveness to its own end, and so the standard needs to be established before the corresponding science can get off the ground.

The end of an Art is given by its "major premise", which declares what is valuable within the Art. Scientific reason, therefore, has no bearing on the arguments of what has value. But this is not to say that reason plays no role whatsoever. All major premises need to be justifiable, and this is only possible because of the existence of more general premises. In other words, an end is only justifiable if the Art is conducive to a more general end, of which there are three. All Arts fall into one of three departments that have their own respective ends, and together comprise what Mill calls the Art of Life (Mill 1974, p. 949). Morality, which is concerned with the Right; Prudence, which is concerned with the Expedient; and Aesthetics, which is concerned with the Beautiful or Noble. The building and medicinal arts are both Arts of Prudence, and therefore only justifiable insofar as they promote the Expedient. When a judge determines if a defendant is guilty or not, she is attempting to promote what is Right. Artists, be they jazz drummers or novelists, are creating works that they (and hopefully others) deem Beautiful. Mill's principles span all three departments, but his most famous, the Principle of Liberty is a moral principle. With these general premises established, it is possible to adjudicate between conflicting practices. If a certain Art's precept, like the use of asbestos in the building Arts, starts to impinge upon another Art, such as medicine, then it is only be appealing to the standard of Expediency to determine which Art must yield, and amend its precepts. However, when a conflict between practices of different departments conflict, then it is only by appealing to an even more general standard that settlements can be made and priorities established.

The Art of Life is governed by one ultimate standard that is the only justification for any particular Art, and is also the ultimate test of all of the rules of human conduct within the three departments. There can be only one standard at this highest level of critical evaluation because several would lead to conflicting evaluations of different Arts. The ultimate standard is, of course, utility:

> . . . the general principle to which all rules of practice ought to conform, and the test by which they should be tried, is that

of conduciveness to the happiness of mankind, or rather, of all
sentient beings: in other words, that the promotion of happiness
is the ultimate principle of Teleology. (Mill 1974, p. 951)

Every Art must ultimately promote general happiness. This is not
to say that every precept of an Art is directed toward happiness;
every precept of an Art is directed toward its own end. But that end
must contribute to the ultimate goal of general happiness. When
the ends of different Arts conflict (or their precepts), it is with this
standard that priorities can be made. Consider the Art of crafting
fiscal policy, which has as its end the economic prosperity of the
country. Economic prosperity is typically considered necessary for
the general happiness of the country. But when fiscal policy achieves
economic prosperity with policies that conflict with other ends, such
as justice, or dignity, then the policies need to be balanced against
these other utility-producing ends. And if many fiscal policies tend
to regularly conflict with these other ends, then the end of fiscal
policy itself, economic prosperity, might need to be revised, or
replaced altogether.

By establishing one standard to measure all Practices or Arts,
Mill posits the linchpin of his entire doctrine. All of his goals for
reform, and all of his principles of morality and government are
all justified because they promote general happiness, supposedly.
The Art of Life has the effect of creating two levels of evaluation
of one's actions. One the first level, when engaging in some Art,
conduct must conform to the rules or precepts of the Art. On the
second level, the Art itself is evaluated in terms of its conduciveness
to general happiness. Conduct itself is not to be assessed in terms of
its direct contribution toward happiness, but only toward the Art's
end. For example, Mill cites the cultivation of a virtuous character
as possibly entailing some pain to oneself, as well to close relations.
But the cultivation may nonetheless be justified, because general
happiness tends to be promoted by an increase of virtue in society.
By proposing a doctrine of all conduct, governed by one principle,
Mill aspires to a coherency and systematization lacking in the
rationalist thinkers that he criticizes. However, as we will discuss
in the last chapter, this aspiration opens Mill up to several different
types of challenges, some which he has been wrestling with during
his lifetime, and some of which have arisen in the recent literature
on his work. Suffice it to say, because of the centrality of the Art of

Life, Mill's entire project of reform turns on its ability adjudicate between competing demands of different Arts. A failure to do this, and Mill's personal, moral, and political prescriptions collapse into a cacophony of competing claims, with no systematic weight over the practices he seeks to replace.

CHAPTER THREE

Revised utilitarianism and justice

One need not stray very far from the epic statement of Mill's scientific method to find it informing his other theories and principles. Mill's moral theory in *Utilitarianism* is largely an inductive project, where he specifically takes to task the intuitive school of ethics as being arbitrary, unsystematic, and ultimately inductive. Only experience can determine the rules of social conduct, specifically experience of what makes people happy. Happiness remains a somewhat nebulous concept in Mill's writings, in part because he conceives of it as a heterogeneous experience that can be associated with practically any end. So, in order to understand how Mill constructs the Art of morality and conduct, justified by the *summum bonum*, it will be necessary first to review how Mill revises the concept of pleasure and happiness, specifically with the challenges of Macaulay and Carlyle in mind. When Mill emerged from his mental crisis, he had two realizations about the nature of happiness: first, it should not be the direct end of action; people must pursue activities for themselves and experience the pleasure and happiness that have come to be associated with the activity. Second, it is not sufficient to accept people as they are and try to satiate their given desires and capacities for pleasure. In order to experience the highest amount and quality of pleasure, people must cultivate their human faculties. Mill's purpose in *Utilitarianism* is in part to work these insights into the Classical Utilitarianism of Bentham and his father.

Qualitative hedonism

Mill was the godson and student of Jeremy Bentham, who is considered one of the key exponents of Classical Utilitarianism. Along with his father, James Mill, John Mill was a member of the Philosophic Radicals, a group of activists and politicians trying to reform the English government, by applying Bentham's utilitarian methods and ideas. Mill absorbed much from Bentham, and so it will be helpful to begin by examining the basics of Bentham's utilitarianism. As Mill grew older, he parted with Bentham on some key points. Bentham was a prolific writer, and describes his principle of utility in several writings. The most systematic exposition of his principle is articulated in *Introduction to the Principles of Morality and Legislation*.

> Nature has placed mankind under the governance of two sovereign masters, *pain* and *pleasure*. It is for them alone to point out what we ought to do, as well as to determine what we shall do. On the one hand the standard of right and wrong, on the other the chain of causes and effects, are fastened to their throne. They govern us in all we do, in all we say, in all we think: every effort we can make to throw off our subjection, will serve but to demonstrate and confirm it. (Bentham 1970, p. 11)

Bentham is clearly articulating a hedonistic version of utilitarianism. Pleasure plays a dual role in Bentham's account: it is simultaneously the sole motivator of all action (psychological hedonism), as well as the *only* ethical standard for making value judgments (normative hedonism). The duality of pleasure in the theory raises the question how it is possible for someone to maximize pleasure generally and impartially if they are only motivated by their own pleasure. Another way to cast this problem is as the inevitable conflict between one's private interests and society's general interests. Bentham does not rely upon any selfless notion of altruism to help promote welfare: an examination of some of his many practical proposals, such as workhouses for the poor, the Panopticon architecture for prisons, or salary bidding for positions in the Civil Service, demonstrates that the key strategy for reform of social and political institutions was to arrange such institutions so that the individual's interests would overlap with society's interests. Bentham defends what he calls the duty-interest junction principle—that managers should do everything in their ability to tie a worker's interests as close as possible to their duties (Bentham 1843, p. 380). In this way, one need not be motivated by anything other than self-interest to promote the welfare of their company, community or country. In order to reform the political system so that everyone's interests could be maximized harmoniously, it is only necessary to know people's sensitivities to pleasure and pain, which are the opposite sides of the same homogeneous conception of utility. It is therefore possible to measure pleasure/pain in terms of its dimensions, such as *intensity*, *duration*, *certainty*, *propinquity* (or remoteness), *fecundity* (or the possibility of leading to more pleasure/pain), *purity* (or the extent to which pain/pleasure is mixed with its opposite), and the *extent* that other people share in the sensation (Bentham 1970, p. 39). The value of a pleasure is directly proportional to its measurement upon these quantitative dimensions. It does not matter what the source of the pleasure is, only the net quantity that is yielded by the activity or policy. As Mill complains, for Bentham "quantity of pleasure being equal, push-pin is as good as poetry"[1] (Mill 1969b, p. 113). A low measure on one of Bentham's metrics, could be compensated by a high measure on any of the others. A mild pleasure could be overall more valuable than a more intense pleasure, if its duration was long enough. These measurements are completely neutral between the sources of pleasure, be they attached to gorging oneself on junk food or reading poetry. Bentham accepted the psychological egoism of human nature and thought that by systematically applying this understanding he could reform all aspects of social and political life.

The Philosophic Radicals, not surprisingly, attracted much criticism, both from those who defended the existing institutions and arrangements, and those who simply thought their proposals were misguided. For example, the Whig politician, Lord Macaulay, attacked James Mill's *Essay on Government* for its attempt to deduce principles of government from the utilitarian premise of psychological hedonism. If all people only desire their own pleasure, it would be absurd to expect the large number of poor people to respect the property rights of the small number of wealthy people. Everyone's long-term interests in maintaining a system of property rights would pale in comparison to the short-term benefit of forcefully redistributing the aristocracy's wealth (Macaulay 1860, p. 311). Macaulay's point is that the rule of law is only possible because individuals habitually forgo what is in their interests, or what is pleasurable, out of a sense of moral obligation. More generally, the static and one-dimensional conception of human nature that underpinned Bentham's system drew the criticisms of the English Romantic, Thomas Carlyle. Carlyle objected to the mechanical approach that Bentham and his followers took to reform: tinkering with external arrangements between people, and neglecting spiritual and moral development. He denied that happiness could be maximized merely by altering the material circumstance of people, and without significant individual struggle (Carlyle 2008, p. 38). Mill accepted these criticisms and incorporated them into his own departures from the Classical Utilitarianism of Bentham and his father. Mill accepted the psychological hedonism of his inherited utilitarianism but understood this law of human nature to be operating at the most fundamental level of mind. What his father and Bentham missed was the fact that through association, the mind was capable of generating desires for goals that were not explicitly connected to pleasure. One of the aims of *Utilitarianism* is to show how virtue and justice are possible, even though humans desire pleasure at the most fundamental level of their minds. This misunderstanding of psychological hedonism manifests itself at the practical level of habit and disposition and was symptomatic of a larger gap in the utilitarian doctrine. Bentham, Mill argues in *Remarks on Bentham's Philosophy*, was too focused on individual behavior, and never sufficiently considered the central role of an individual's character or disposition. By doing so, Bentham neglected a primary cause of both criminal and beneficent behavior (Mill 1969a, p. 7). Moreover, by focusing primarily on external actions,

> Man is never recognized by [Bentham] as a being capable of pursuing spiritual perfection as an end; of desiring, for its own sake, the conformity of his own character to his standard of excellence, without hope or fear of evil from other source than his own inward consciousness. (Mill 1969b, p. 95)

Bentham was, admittedly, more interested in reforming the law and policy, than morality or personal cultivation. But by doing so, the Philosophic Radicals limited the full potential of utilitarianism.

Their critiques of the existing institutions were powerful, but in order to make utilitarianism the foundation of political, cultural, and personal reform, Mill would have to provide a more nuanced conception of human nature that could account for the myriad of valuable goals and commitments that seem at odds with the dual role of pleasure.

Utilitarianism is one of the main vehicles for addressing the challenges to Mill's inherited doctrine. At the outset, Mill declares his commitment to the standard of utility like his predecessors, but he immediately clarifies utility in such a way to assuage the concerns of utilitarianism's critics. The foundation of morality for Mill is that "actions are right in proportion as they tend to promote happiness, wrong as they tend to produce the reverse of happiness. By happiness is intended pleasure, and the absence of pain; by unhappiness, pain, and the privation of pleasure" (Mill 1969c, p. 210). As the standard that evaluates and justifies all actions, the Principle of Utility is the very same principle that governs the Art of Life, in its three departments, Morality, Prudence, and Aesthetics, as described at the end of *A System of Logic*. The Principle of Utility is based on Mill's first principle, or his Theory of Life, as he calls it in *Utilitarianism*, which states that pleasure and absence of pain are the only desirable ends; in other words, pleasure is the only value. (I will henceforth only refer to "happiness" in reference to the utilitarian end, and "pleasure" as those objects and pursuits that make up happiness.) Principles that make happiness their primary object have existed since the Epicureans, more than 2000 years ago. And for as long, Mill claims, such attempts have drawn criticism for placing such a pedestrian and base experience at the heart of morality. Such critics, like Carlyle, accuse the followers of this principle to be peddling a "doctrine worthy only of swine" (Mill 1969c, p. 210). Mill retorts that it is not utilitarians but their detractors who disparage human nature when they liken the pleasures of humans to those of swine. Humans, with their "elevated faculties" are capable of enjoying a far greater range of pleasures than pigs. In fact, Classical Utilitarians, though formally neutral between sources of pleasure, have nonetheless prioritized the pleasures of the mind over the body, not because of any inherent superiority, but for circumstantial reasons, because of their "greater permanency, safety, uncostliness . . . " (Mill 1969c, p. 211). And this very point is one of the key departures for Mill from his classical predecessors. For Mill, there *are* inherent qualities that distinguish pleasures from each other, and it would be absurd not to take that into account when calculating net pleasure:

> Of two pleasures, if there be one to which all or almost all who have experience of both give a decided preference, irrespective of any feeling of moral obligation to prefer it, that is the more desirable pleasure. If one of the two is, by those who are competently acquainted with both, placed so far above the other that they prefer it, even knowing it to be attended with a greater amount of discontent, and would not resign it for any quantity of the other pleasure which their nature is capable of, we are justified in ascribing to the preferred enjoyment a superiority in quality so far outweighing quantity as to render it, in comparison, in small amount. (Mill 1969c, p. 211)

Mill's revision of Bentham's conception of pleasure is two-fold: first, that pleasure varies in quality, and second, that the class of higher pleasures is incommensurably superior to the class of lower pleasures. This latter distinction is necessary to ensure that the utilitarian legislator always prioritizes the sorts of activities that people like Carlyle value over the sensual pleasures of people (and swine). If an increasingly larger amount of the lower pleasure could eventually be equal to or greater than the value of a higher pleasure, then the utilitarian legislator might be tempted to pursue policies that promoted the lower pleasures (e.g. because of cheapness, or simplicity), at the expense of the higher ones. But since there is no common unit of pleasure between them, the superiority of the higher pleasures can never be outweighed by increasing any of the dimensions of the lower ones. This introduction of different qualities to pleasure is not only a radical move away from the homogeneous conception of pleasure that Bentham and the Classical Utilitarians held, it is also potentially a departure from hedonism altogether.

For all versions of hedonism, pleasure is the only source of a value, and hence the more pleasure an action produces, as measured by Bentham's metrics, the more value it possesses. Bentham's metrics provide cardinal measurements, so a deficiency in any one dimension (e.g. intensity), could be compensated for by any of the other dimensions (e.g. duration). But with the distinction between higher and lower pleasures, Mill introduces a new dimension, that of quality. The dimension of quality is unique because high measurements of any of the other dimensions cannot compensate for a pleasure being low. By "higher", Mill means that a pleasure is infinitely superior to the lower ones, because no amount of a lower pleasure can ever be preferable to any amount of the higher pleasure. In other words, the assessment of quality produces incommensurable and ordinal rankings of pleasure. It is reasonable to claim that pleasure is not as uniform and homogeneous as Bentham and the Classical Utilitarians conceive, or even that some pleasures are superior in value to others. But Mill's claim is far stronger—that higher pleasures are so fundamentally superior to lower ones, as to render questions of quantity irrelevant when comparing the two. But if this qualitative distinction exists between pleasures, then it is not clear what is it that makes the higher pleasure fundamentally more *valuable*, if not more *pleasure*?

Mill cites the higher faculties of the human mind to explain the qualitative superiority of the higher pleasures. Understanding, intellectual and aesthetic contemplation, sympathy for others (beyond one's family) are some of the faculties that separate humans from animals, and require cultivation to fully utilize. But once a person has achieved a critical level of development, the exercise of these faculties becomes infinitely more pleasurable than the satisfaction of sensual desires. Apart from circumstantial reasons (e.g. addiction), one would never resign the exercise of the human faculties in favor of the gratification of sensual desires. In fact, so superior are the higher pleasures, that merely possessing the *un*exercised capacity to experience the higher pleasures would still be preferable to the satisfaction of all of one's sensual desires. The frustration of desires for the higher pleasures leaves one susceptible to experiencing more complex pain and "acute suffering," but nonetheless, "It is better to be a human being dissatisfied than a pig satisfied; better to be Socrates dissatisfied than a fool satisfied" (Mill 1969c, p. 212). To claim that a state of dissatisfaction can be preferable over a state of satisfaction would seem to violate the fundamental first principle of utilitarianism, but for Mill there is a special dignity connected to the exercise of the human faculties that causes one to make such a valuation. As will be discussed below, far from being a violation of hedonism, the disinterested purist of virtue is central to Mill's strategy of maximizing general happiness. Virtuous people are a source of much benevolence in the world, but are also instrumental to helping other people develop their own characters and human faculties. Once a person becomes capable of appreciating the higher pleasures, they are endowed with informal authority to identify such pleasures to the uninitiated. To be clear, it is not that the "competent judges" ordain certain pleasures as higher; instead, the competent judges, with their fully developed human faculties, are capable of identifying the higher pleasures and so can help discover them. By connecting the higher pleasures to human faculties and ultimately to dignity, Mill is attempting to illustrate the heterogeneous and hierarchical nature of pleasure. The question is whether it is coherent to have radically incommensurable aspects to pleasure, or if Mill is really describing something other than pleasure.

Mill received much criticism over his qualitative distinction between pleasures from his initial commentators, such as G. E. Moore in his *Principia Ethica* (Moore 1962, p. 79). The charge is that by accepting the utilitarian Theory of Life, Mill is committed to pleasure being the only desirable end. As the only "currency" of value, a larger amount of pleasure must be more valuable than a smaller amount of pleasure (as measured by Bentham's metrics). But by introducing qualitative differences of pleasure, whereby a smaller amount of higher pleasure is more valuable than a larger amount of lower pleasure, Mill has imported a new "currency" of value, of which the higher pleasure has more. Moore concludes, either Mill must give up the qualitative distinction between pleasures, and concede that a large enough amount of lower pleasure can be more valuable than a small amount of higher pleasure, or Mill must give up the hedonistic commitment to pleasure being the sole source of value (Moore 1962, p. 81). Since these early critiques, there have been many scholars who have endeavored to present a more sympathetic revision of Mill's hedonism. Roger Crisp defends Mill's hedonistic credentials by describing the higher/lower distinction as yet another property of pleasure, like its duration, intensity, etc. (Crisp 1997, p. 34). As a pleasure of eight minutes is preferable to one of three minutes, so too is a higher pleasure preferable to lower one. More time does not in itself alter the nature of the value, nor does the fact that the pleasure exercises the higher human faculties. However, when these dimensions are of pleasure, they affect its net value. It is still only pleasure that we are describing, and so Mill can remain safely within the confines of hedonism. The nature (whether it is higher or lower) of a pleasure may be yet another dimension of it, but Crisp does not account for its uniquely *in*commensurating effect. Whereas the duration of a pleasure may compensate for its lack of intensity, nothing can compensate for it being of a lower quality. The nature of the pleasure sets it apart in a way that its other properties do not, and it is unclear how hedonism can accommodate this transformative dimension. John Plamenatz and Jonathan Riley analogize pleasure with color.[2] If color is the only good, and a person were to then rank the colors in order of beauty, she would not be importing any new value to do so. To rank colors is not to admit any other good, apart from color, because that is the only dimension in which they vary. Similarly, to rank pleasure with respect to quality is to do so using only pleasure and nothing else. However, it is one thing to rank colors, or pleasures, with respect to one's preferences, it is another thing to declare that some colors are inherently and categorically more valuable. Whereas the former is an empirical statement about preference, the latter is a normative claim regarding value, or what every rational person's ranking *should be*, and therefore must be justified with reference to some criterion—duration, intensity, etc. Remember, Mill's claim is that no amount of the lower can ever rival the higher, that is, no incremental increases in quantity can be made to make the lower pleasure higher. Whereas color can gradually shift from one to another, and pleasure can shift from one length to another, the nature of a pleasure cannot, according to Mill. There is a discontinuity in value between higher and lower pleasures, and if Bentham's dimensions of pleasure cannot bridge the divide, then the nature of a pleasure is a unique dimension that measures a value distinct from pleasure itself. The analogies that these interpretations employ are incapable of accounting for the radical incommensurability between the different qualities of pleasure.

Whether consistent with hedonism or not, the qualitative superiority of some pleasures is necessary for Mill's liberal-utilitarian doctrine. As Carlyle charged, Bentham sought primarily institutional reforms to alleviate suffering, and neglected personal and spiritual considerations. Classical Utilitarian's homogeneous conception of pleasure implies that there is no inherent superiority in striving to appreciate more elevated pleasures. Expressing one's individuality— for Mill, the source of the highest pleasures—holds no privileged place over conforming to one's peers, and could even be an obstacle

to maximizing pleasure overall. Bentham's various institutional
reforms, and his application of the duty-interest junction principle,
makes clear that for him harmonizing people's interests is the key to
maximization of pleasure. Mill, on the other hand, posits a conception
of human nature that must express itself, while at the same time
must be channeled into projects that develop one's human faculties.
Mill's description of the higher pleasures as utilizing the human
faculties and the 'capacity for nobler feelings' is a restatement of his
depiction of individuality in *On Liberty*. Even though not explicitly
argued in terms of pleasure, Mill's valuation of individuality in the
contemporaneously conceived essay can only be because of it being
a source of more and *higher* pleasures. As with the capacities for
the higher pleasures, the need for individuality is generic. In *On
Liberty*, Mill speaks of inward forces (Mill 1977b, p. 263), energy
(p. 263), pagan self-assertion (p. 266), and personal impulse (p. 264)
within all humans and necessitating the social and political space
for expression. And also like the capacity to experience the higher
pleasures, individuality needs to be developed over time, and can
wither in an oppressive and hostile environment. Finally, cultivating
the human faculties that enable the higher pleasures is a social
endeavor for most people, relying on the assistance of competent
judges. Likewise in *On Liberty*, informal authority is conferred to
social elites to dis-incentivize behavior that is at odds with Mill's
ideal of individual and social reform. Mill is not simply trying to
maximize the satisfaction of peoples' desires for pleasure, he is trying
to change their desires altogether. Hence, at the core of Mill's liberal-
utilitarian doctrine, with all of its subsidiary projects, is the necessity
to develop one's character. The introspective, and possibly difficult
cultivation of one's character would enable one to experience the
higher pleasures that best conform to one's individual nature. Mill's
developmental and Romantic version of utilitarianism is a necessary
departure from the more mechanistic and static utilitarianism of
Bentham and the Radicals, in order to move from criticizing existing
institutions to providing an ideal, around which to orient reform.

The "proof" of utilitarianism

Part of the reason for revising the utilitarian conception of happiness
is to make clear that the specific content of the utilitarian morality

is not very different than customary morality. *Utilitarianism* is an attempt to demonstrate that from the standard of happiness, the same range of moral rules and rights as those that are purported to have come from God or moral intuition can be deduced, with the added advantage of being more systematic. As with his epistemology and conception of the self, Mill is attempting to expose the fact that intuitive morality is often really learned morality. Mill acknowledges that moral intuitionists do often appeal to general moral principles, however none distill their principles down to a "common source of obligation," or first principle (Mill 1969c, p. 206). Lacking a *summum bonum*, intuitionists often implicitly defer to experience in an ad hoc manner in order to establish moral rules.

> Although the non-existence of an acknowledged first principle has made ethics not so much a guide as a consecration of men's actual sentiments, still, as men's sentiments, both of favour and of aversion, are greatly influenced by what they suppose to be the effects of things upon their happiness, the principle of utility, or as Bentham latterly called it, the greatest happiness principle, has had a large share in forming the moral doctrines even of those who most scornfully reject its authority. (Mill 1969c, p. 207)

These facts would seem to complicate Mill's project in *Utilitarianism*: he is trying to propose a new system of morality that is largely the same as what people accept as customary, is governed by a standard that people already use, and yet, is attacked by both liberal and conservative critics as being revolutionary (Wilson 1990, p. 5). Instead, Mill builds these observations of how people practice morality into his much maligned "proof" of utilitarianism. As Mill concedes in several places in *Utilitarianism*, as well as in the last chapter of *A System of Logic*, ultimate ends, or first principles of any practice (e.g. morality) cannot be proved in the ordinary sense. However, the adoption or rejection of first principles is not an arbitrary decision. "There is a larger meaning of the word proof," for which evidence can be supplied and reasons given for the mind to consider (Mill 1969c, p. 208). Mill's proof in *Utilitarianism* is best understood as proceeding in three broad steps: first, he provides evidence that happiness is the only end, second, he extrapolates from this evidence to show that general happiness is the only end, and, most crucially, third, he argues that anything desired other than happiness, can only be as a means to happiness (Crisp 1997, p. 72).[3] With regard to this last step, Mill is especially concerned to show that the desirability of virtue, often cited as evidence against the Principle of Utility, is actually compatible with it. Mill's proof has attracted much attention in the secondary literature. I will limit myself to highlighting the most controversial parts.

Step 1

Mill needs to show that happiness is an end, and is the only end, and his strategy is to show that happiness is desirable. Some of the criticism surrounding Mill's proof focuses on the ambiguity in the English language of the word "desirable." Mill begins by stating, "Questions about ends are, in other words, questions what things are desirable" (Mill 1969c, p. 234). Mill employs the word "desirable" seemingly in the normative sense of the word, as in what should be desired. However the only evidence that Mill provides is that people actually desire it, in the descriptive sense.

> The only proof capable of being given that an object is visible, is that people actually see it. The only proof that sound is audible, is that people hear it . . . In like manner, I apprehend, the sole evidence it is possible to produce that anything is desirable, is that people do actually desire it. (Ibid.)

This move, using the word "desirable" in its two senses interchangeably is one of the problematic steps Mill takes in his proof. It suggests he confuses two very different uses of the word desirable. Whereas words like "visible" and "audible" only have a descriptive sense, words like "desirable" and "lovable" tend to only have a normative sense. Moore, refers to this as the "Naturalistic Fallacy"—simply put, Mill apparently makes a normative conclusion from a descriptive premise (Moore 1962, p. 66). Mill's use of the ambiguous term has largely been defended in the subsequent literature, because in previous writings, Mill makes clear that "A proposition of which the predicate is expressed by the words ought or should be, is generally different from one which is expressed by is, or will be"[4] (Mill 1974, p. 949). Moreover, Mill expressly states that questions of ultimate ends, or first principles, are not susceptible to proof in the traditional sense, so his strategy is to supply the only *evidence* available to support the normative claim, which is to demonstrate the truth of the descriptive claim that people actually do desire happiness. That happiness is desired by people is for sure an uncontroversial claim, but it is a necessary one because "If the end which the utilitarian doctrine proposes to itself were not, in theory and in practice, acknowledged to be an end, nothing could ever convince any person that is was so" (Mill 1969c, p. 234). In other words, Mill would have had a much tougher sell, if no one, in fact, did desire happiness. However meager, that some people desire happiness is simply the only evidence that he can provide, given his epistemological commitments to empiricism. Though Mill's use of the word desirable seems ambiguous, the real confusion of this step is with Mill's use of the term "proof." Mill is not proving anything here because, as he readily admits, such a proof is not possible. He is merely providing the only legitimate evidence open to him for his argument that happiness should be the end of all action, which is that there is empirical evidence of people desiring it.

Step 2

Mill has thusly supplied evidence for the claim that happiness is the desirable end in the normative sense. The next step for Mill is to show that everyone's happiness is in fact desirable (in the normative sense), and so is the true end of utilitarianism. Mill makes this move rather quickly, relying once again on the uncontroversial fact that individuals desire their own happiness.

> No reason can be given why the general happiness is desirable, except that each person . . . desires his own happiness. This, however, being a fact, we have not only all the proof which the case admits of, but all which is possible to require, that happiness is a good: that each person's happiness is a good to that person, and the general happiness, therefore, a good to the aggregate of all persons. (Ibid.)

This passage can be understood in two ways. The first is that the fact that each person desires their own happiness (in the descriptive sense) is evidence that everyone's happiness is therefore desirable (in the normative sense). This understanding of the passage is considered a *fallacy of composition*. It could just as likely be the case that the selfish egoist can accept that his desiring happiness is evidence of the desirability of his happiness, but reject the desirability of other people's happiness. And aggregating this type of person would yield a society of individuals all attaching the same value to their own happiness, but none to anyone else's. A second way to understand passage is supported by a footnote in Chapter V of *Utilitarianism* where Mill addresses this very point. In defending the demand of impartiality at the heart of the Principle of Utility, Mill clarifies that the Principle "may be more correctly described as supposing that equal amounts of happiness are equally desirable, whether felt by the same or by different persons" (Mill 1969c, p. 258). Based on this clarification, a better understanding of the passage is that the fact that each desires their own happiness is evidence of the value of happiness, not just to that person but to everyone. This much more modest claim avoids the fallacy of composition by stopping short of transforming the aggregation of everyone's respective valuation of their own happiness into the inherent value of the aggregation of everyone's happiness. Hence, if we aggregate everyone's respective valuation of their own happiness, then this aggregation is merely *evidence* of the inherent value of aggregate happiness. It does not prove it. Much like in step 1, Mill is saying that there is no other evidence that can be offered for the desirability of general happiness, other than the fact that individuals desire their own happiness. This evidence is obviously much weaker for supporting the wider claim about the desirability of general happiness. Mill might have also provided as evidence the fact that many people do value other people's happiness equally or even greater than their own, such as in the case of love. Mill does think that eventually there will come a point in history when the organization of society and education will shape individuals to value their own happiness truly impartially (Mill 1972, p. 1414). He calls this period the Religion of Humanity (Mill 1969e, p. 422). This future state of affairs would constitute even more evidence of the normative desirability of general happiness, but of course, still not prove it in the ordinary sense. In light of the limited nature of Mill's claim, and the overwhelming evidence for it, the burden of proof is actually on the selfish egoist to show that their happiness alone has value, but that others' happiness do not. Mill must make do with the only evidence available to him for the unprovable claim about the desirability of general happiness, however weak.

Step 3

Mill relies solely on the empirical evidence that people desire their own happiness. This fact is the only evidence possible to support the argument that happiness is desirable in the normative sense. The modesty of the first two steps makes the third step all the more difficult. People clearly seem to desire things other than their own happiness, or even general happiness; why is this not evidence that goals other than happiness are also desirable? Some pursuits distinct from happiness clearly are means to happiness, such as wealth or political power. But don't individuals sometimes sacrifice their own happiness for entirely different ends, like virtue? As Lord Macaulay argues in his critique of Classical Utilitarianism, if people only desired and pursued their own happiness, then there would be no way to secure allegiance to the law when it impedes individual happiness. People would only follow the law or be equitable with others when it was compatible with their own interests. Hence, Mill takes special care to explicate how the Principle of Utility is capable of accounting for the desirability of virtue for itself, and not only as means to happiness.

Virtuous behavior, as a means to some other end, is by definition not virtuous. Virtue is an autonomous quality that is an end in itself, despite its positive or negative consequences. Bravery is a virtue not because it promotes happiness (although it often does) but because it is simply admirable, even when it is vein. It is therefore quite a challenge for Mill to accommodate virtue within the Principle of Utility, while at the same time maintaining the autonomy of virtue as desirable in itself and not as a means to happiness. The first half of this effort can derive some support from *A System of Logic*, where Mill clarifies that the Principle of Utility does not demand that general happiness be the end of every action:

> I do not mean to assert that the promotion of happiness should be itself the end of all actions, or even of the rules of action. It is the justification, and ought to be the controller, of all ends, but is not itself the sole end. There are many virtuous actions, and even modes of action (though the cases are, I think, less frequent than is often supposed) by which happiness in the particular instance is sacrificed, more pain being produced than pleasure. But conduct of which this can be truly asserted, admits

of justification only because it can be shown that on the whole more happiness will exist in the world, if feelings are cultivated which will make people, in certain cases, regardless of happiness. (Mill 1974, p. 952)

Here Mill justifies the desirability of virtue from the standpoint of the Principle of Utility, by recognizing that an increasing stock of virtuous people will promote general happiness. And in *Utilitarianism*, Mill also states that virtue is at the very head of things that are good as means to the ultimate end (Mill 1969c, p. 235). But if virtuous behavior does promote general happiness, can such behavior really be considered virtuous? Mill says yes, because when people pursue virtuous behavior they do so without regard for its beneficial consequences; in other words, they desire virtue for itself. To understand how, we must return to the laws of associationist psychology. One of the laws is that when two sensory impressions have been experienced together, they tend to become associated with each other. Hence, when two impressions become associated, stimulating or recalling one impression will result in experiencing the other. Another law is that when two or more ideas become strongly associated, they can become inseparable in the mind (Mill 1974, p. 853). Mill describes how money is not desired because people want to possess coins and notes; instead money, like fame and power, is desired because of its instrumental value for pleasure. Eventually, the association between money and pleasure will lead to money being desired for itself, independent of the desire to spend it to obtain pleasure. What associationist psychology reveals is that once the pursuit of an object becomes associated with pleasure, the association can become deep and obscure, such that the person does not consciously have happiness in mind, when pursuing the associated object. Likewise, virtue, originally desired as a means to happiness, once associated with it, becomes desired for itself. Is this not pursuing virtuous behavior for the sake of happiness, and so not really virtue? Not so, if we understand virtue to be a complex idea, produced by the chemical association between some virtuous actions and pleasure. A chemical, as opposed to mechanical, association is when several ideas dissolve into each other, thereby creating a distinctly new idea. The process yields a complex idea whereby the antecedent ideas are no longer identifiable in the new one. If we understand virtue as such a complex idea, we can see how the individual does not consciously desire happiness when pursuing virtue, and yet accept that the desire for virtue only exists because of the obscured link to pleasure. Mill argues that many of the ingredients of happiness have such a relationship with pleasure.

Many scholars remain skeptical of Mill's hedonistic account of virtue.[5] Either the pursuit of virtue is for itself, and not a means to happiness, in which case Mill must accept that people desire things other than happiness and that these things are also valuable, or virtue is desired as a means to happiness, in which case it's not really virtue. Even if we grant Mill's psychological account of how individuals come to desire virtue, it is reasonable to question whether it conforms to Mill's Theory of Life and respects the non-hedonistic value of virtue. In all three steps, we see Mill appealing to observation and experience to supply evidence for arguments that are philosophical and logical in nature. Mill makes a similar "naturalizing" move with his justification of inductive reasoning in *A System of Logic*. There, as in here, we see Mill appealing to the only source of evidence he accepts, experience.

Sanctions

Happiness may seem an unlikely standard for morality, because it is commonly thought that a person's individual happiness is independent of the demands of morality. But whether or not one accepts happiness as the ultimate standard of morality, Mill points out that one's happiness is usually one of the largest considerations when determining right and wrong action (Mill 1969c, p. 207). An important point that Mill stresses is that his utilitarian doctrine is not as radical as is commonly charged, and actually overlaps with much of the morality that people would consider customary. This fact is especially true with regard to the sanctions that compel people to follow moral rules. A fundamental question for any code of behavior is "why obey it?" This question is often skeptically posed to people trying to propose a new standard, but it is equally applicable to all systems of morality and ethics. The reason for this skepticism is that moral rules are generally socialized into individuals by formative institutions, like the family, schools, and religion. This explicit and implicit instilling of morality into young children leads them to feel that the rules are self-evident, and not derived from a general principle. Utilitarianism might some day become the customary morality, at which point all of the powers of formative institutions would be directed toward instilling *its* rules of behavior into individuals, in which case they would feel obligatory *in themselves*. Until then, utilitarianism, like all systems of morality, must rely upon "enforcers" to compel continuing obedience to its maxims. These sanctions are either external, in that they are derived from society, or internal, originating in the mind. The external sanctions are twofold, the first being the desire to be held in a positive regard by other people. Vanity is a powerful motive of behavior, and breaking customary norms of behavior is one way to alienate oneself from others. The second external sanction is the fear of God, which is a powerful regulator of behavior, independent of self-interest. These external sanctions are not specific to any particular system of morality, and so could be brought to bear on the utilitarian morality just as effectively as any other. For example, Mill plausibly argues that the greatest happiness for the greatest number of people is exactly what a benevolent God would command. But as effective as these external sanctions are, Mill is much more concerned with the internal sanction of morality, which has also been brought to bear on many different standards of morality.

The internal sanction is the pain one feels when violating a moral rule, and the pleasure of conforming to it. Mill calls this sense of duty, conscience, and he stresses that the of this sanction are varied and complex. It is the culmination of the sum total of a person's experiences, being derived "from sympathy, from love, and still more from fear; from all the forms of religious feeling; from the recollections of childhood and of all our past life; from self-esteem, desire of the esteem of others, and occasionally even from self-abasement" (Mill 1969c, p. 228). Mill does not give a full psychological account of the development of conscience, but the laws of association that govern the mind make possible attachment of this sanction to any moral rule. For example, morality derived from "transcendent sources"—by which, Mill references Kantian ethics—are subject to the same psychological laws as learned morality, and so are enforced by the same sanction of conscience. There is no additional metaphysical motivation to obey. At this point in the argument, it would seem utilitarian ethics, or any other for that matter, holds no privileged place in human psychology. The internal sanction of conscience can be cultivated in any direction, attaching itself to any system of morality. Mill has not yet explained why one should adopt the utilitarian ethic over others. Interestingly, rather than rest upon the utilitarian Theory of Life , that pleasure is the only valuable end, Mill makes a psychological argument about the appropriateness of directing the internal sanction of conscience toward general happiness.

> . . . there *is* this basis of powerful natural sentiment; and this it is which, when once the general happiness is recognized as the ethical standard, will constitute the strength of the utilitarian morality. This firm foundation is that of social feelings of mankind; the desire to be in unity with our fellow creatures, which is already a powerful principle in human nature, and happily one of those which tend to become stronger, even without express inculcation, from the influences of advancing civilization. (Mill 1969c, p. 231)

Man being a social creature tends toward socialization, which naturally entails the consideration of the interests of others. This natural sentiment provides the basis for the cultivation of the conscience toward the utilitarian ethic, and it becomes incumbent upon society to establish institutions that foster this particular moral development. This grounding of the utilitarian morality in human nature is plausible because observation reveals overwhelming evidence of humans living in social groups. And as civilization progresses, it reinforces this sentiment. Ultimately, this progression leads to the Religion of Humanity, the period of history when all of the political and cultural institutions of society instill and reinforce a complete impartiality between one's interests and those of everyone else. (Mill 1969e, p. 422). Fear of God is replaced by love of humanity, as the distinction between the external and internal sanctions would fade away. The social and psychological enforcements of right and wrong are the same for all moral codes. Where utilitarianism has the edge over others, according to Mill, is with it cohering better with the natural tendencies within individuals to live in the society of others.

Justice

The last topic Mill takes up in *Utilitarianism* is the utilitarian conception of justice. Here, Mill's goal is to dispel the notion that justice for utilitarianism is a matter of simple expediency, or pursuing pleasure, in an ad hoc manner, and is at odds with what people consider to be the conventional demands of justice. Again, we see Mill stresses that for the most part, the utilitarian conception of justice largely overlaps with customary conceptions of justice, even though it is based on the Principle of Utility. The challenge for Mill is to show that justice is in fact based on the Principle of Utility but not equivalent to it. Mill's explication of the utilitarian conception of justice is intertwined with a formal discussion of morality. Before differentiating these two related concepts, it will be necessary to first understand how Mill accounts for the evolution of the sentiment of justice in the modern human mind. What we see is that the internal sanction of conscience not only serves to enforce morality and justice, it also defines it.

Mill understands humans to be a part of the animal kingdom, and as such share some of the primitive instincts that govern animal behavior. Self-defense and sympathy are two such instincts that are identifiable in the motives of people's behavior, despite the evolution of self-consciousness and intelligence. In fact, these human capacities have modified the instincts of self-defense and sympathy in such a way as to turn them into moral sentiments, or the internal sanction. Whereas animals will retaliate if they, their young, or their kin (the other creatures with whom they can sympathize) are attacked; humans are capable of expanding the scope of their sympathy to ever wider groups, ultimately sympathizing with all of humanity. Moreover, humans are capable of conceiving a wider range of individual and communal interests that go beyond mere bodily integrity and material security. For example, the desire to retaliate will spontaneously emerge within our minds when a company fails to pay its employees the agreed wages, or when the government censors the local newspaper. The desire to retaliate, being natural and rooted in animalistic instincts is not in itself moral. What converts these instincts into moral sentiments is controlling them, so that they are only allowed to motivate us to act in utility-producing ways.

> The sentiment [of justice], in itself, has nothing moral in it; what is moral is, the exclusive subordination of it to the social sympathies, so as to wait on and obey their call. For the natural feeling [desire to retaliate] tends to make us resent indiscriminately whatever

any one does that is disagreeable to us; but when moralized by the social feeling, it only acts in the directions comfortable to the general good: just persons resenting a hurt to society, though not otherwise a hurt to themselves, and not resenting a hurt to themselves, however painful, unless it be of a kind in which society has a common interest with them in the repression of. (Mill 1969c, p. 249)

Individuals might naturally feel the desire to retaliate, or resentment, in response to any action that is contrary to their preferences. The desire might spontaneously emerge when one's favorite sporting team loses, or when an investment one makes in a company is lost. This sentiment (the desire to retaliate) is not moral because it is conducive to the general happiness that sporting teams be able to compete freely, and that investors incur risk. However, if the opposing team won only by cheating, or if our investment was lost because the company engaged in fraud, then it would be moral not only for the sporting fan and business person to feel the desire to retaliate, but for all people to desire retaliation. If the Principle of Utility ultimately moralizes the primitive desire to retaliate, then how are we to know when the desire to retaliate promotes the general happiness?

As human society has evolved from its primitive stages to its current level of organization, the animal impulses within humans become socialized and attach themselves to certain rules that have been beneficial for the group to obey. As the instinct of self-defense (i.e. the desire to retaliate), which is triggered when an individual is attacked, reiterates itself in the social context, the expectation that evil should meet with evil becomes established, and the norm of desert is born. Once the norm of desert is established, the expectation is that evil is met with evil, and good met with good. Then, when someone requests help, but fails to reciprocate when called upon, she fails to meet reasonable or implied expectations, and violates an acknowledged contract, which also triggers the same desire to retaliate. And since all who do good should receive good, and all who do evil should receive evil, we have no reason to treat people prejudicially or partially. This rule is the "first of judicial virtues" according to Mill (Mill 1969c, p. 257). Impartiality and the closely related standard of equality are necessary to oblige the other rules and are at the heart of the utilitarian principle.

When any of these norms of justice are violated, two elements are implied: that a moral wrong has been committed that threatens the security of everyone, and that there is a definite victim. As Mill attempts to show in his "proof" utilitarianism, individuals value their own happiness equally, and so everyone's happiness is equally valuable. No one's happiness is inherently more important or more valuable than anyone else's. At the start of Mill's discussion of justice, he surveys the customary obligations of justice, and we see that they are the same rules that have evolved from the primitive instincts of self-defense and sympathy (legal rights, moral rights, desert, keeping faith, impartiality, and equality). The rules that comprise justice are natural, and have their roots in the primitive desire to defend selfish interests, namely that of security. Originally, these desires were instincts, and motivated by narrow and short-term considerations of expediency. But as society has grown more complex and cooperative, and as primitive instincts defend a wider range of interests and people, the desire to retaliate against a personal offense becomes subordinated to the desire to retaliate against social offenses, and the internal sanction of conscience is born. Empirically, the desire to retaliate is aroused in response to all sorts of personal offenses and set-backs to one's interests, but only the Principle of Utility can determine if the desire is properly moral. Mill's presumption is that as mankind develops, the desire to retaliate will only be aroused for set-backs to social interests, and not simply personal ones. As Mill puts it, "the idea of justice supposes two things; a rule of conduct, and a sentiment which sanctions the rule" (Mill 1969c, p. 249). As we will see, this sentiment, which is at its heart the socialized desire to punish certain actions, constitutes the formal criterion of moral wrongness. The sentiment also differentiates justice from mere expediency. Mill's discussion of justice is intertwined with comments about morality in general. It will therefore be helpful to understand the formal distinctions he makes between positive law, justice, morality, and expediency.

Law vs justice

Mill's survey of the customary obligations of justice, at the start of the chapter is intended to demonstrate that at the core of the concept of justice is the notion of law. But as far back as the Ancient

Greeks and Romans, it was understood that humans, being fallible, sometimes make bad laws.

> And hence the sentiment of injustice came to be attached, not to all violations of law, but only to violations of such laws as *ought* to exist, including such as ought to exist but do not; and to laws themselves, if supposed to be contrary to what ought to be the law. (Mill 1969c, p. 245)

Here Mill makes the important point that the categories of justice and positive law do not overlap perfectly. The violation of a law might be unjust, but obedience to a bad law might also be unjust. Mill clarifies that obligations of justice are more numerous than the obligations of positive law, but there might be good reasons for limiting the scope of law.

> Nobody desires that laws should interfere with the whole detail of private life; yet every one allows that in all daily conduct a person may and does show himself to be either just or unjust. (Ibid.)

This passage makes the crucial point that the area of positive law established by the state should be smaller than the area of justice. Illegal actions are unjust (assuming positive law itself to be just), but there will be some unjust actions that are nonetheless allowed by law. In these instances, when it would be inappropriate for the law to mete out punishment, society should morally condemn the offender. For example, cheating at tennis might be an unjust practice, but to hold the cheater legally responsible, and then bring the full force of the legal and penal system against them would be absurd. The costs of preventing, investigating, and prosecuting such offenses would far outweigh the benefits of legally protecting against such offenses. However, it must be noted that the calculation of whether to criminalize unjust behavior or not is a fluid one: as police technology improves, as well as society's scientific understanding of the harmful consequences of unjust behavior expands, society may come to a different calculation. For example, second hand cigarette smoke in public spaces was originally considered inconsiderate and bothersome, but legally permissible. Recently, science has revealed its harmful effects to nonsmokers, and so has tipped the balance of policy from tolerance toward prohibition in public spaces, in many countries.

Justice vs morality

If positive law and justice represent the rules that govern the interactions between people in social groups, then it remains to distinguish such rules from the larger category of rules—morality.

> Justice is a name for certain classes of moral rules, which concern the essentials of human well-being more nearly, and are therefore of more absolute obligation, than any other rules for the guidance of life . . . (Mill 1969c, p. 255)

In order to understand of what the class of moral rules that concern human well-being (or happiness) consist, Mill describes two different types of moral obligations. All people have duties to obey both perfect and imperfect obligations. Justice is the name of all those perfect obligations or rules that protect the vital interests of people in society. They correlate to rights that everyone possesses and that everyone else must respect. Reviewing the evolution of justice from the instincts of self-esteem and sympathy, we can see how individuals come to possess rights in the security of their persons and possessions. And as the patterns of "expectations" described above, become norms of justice, they too become guaranteed by rights. Imperfect obligations, on the other hand, do not generate any corresponding rights. They are moral rules that allow for individual discretion as to when and how to fulfill; Mill cites the obligation of charity. All people are generally obliged to be charitable, but no particular person or organization has a right to our charity. Stinginess is certainly not morally praiseworthy, but neither is it unjust, because it does not violate anyone's rights.

> Justice implies something which it is not only right to do, and wrong not to do, but which some individual person can claim from us as his moral right. No one has a right to our generosity or beneficence, because we are not morally bound to practice those virtues towards any given individual . . . Wherever there is a right, the case is one of justice, and not of the virtue of beneficence: and whoever does not place the distinction between justice and morality in general where we have now placed it, will be found to make no distinction between them at all, but to merge all morality in justice. (Mill 1969c, p. 247)

Mill places the distinction between the range of justice and the remaining range of morality at exactly this point—where the rules of society are so essential for general happiness that they are enshrined in rights. He takes special care not to assimilate beneficence into perfect obligations because that would be far too demanding, and ultimately self-defeating. The system of acknowledged rights is therefore the product of the sentiment of justice. Rights connect individuals' interests in having the rules of society followed (security, desert, contracts, etc.) to society's general interest in happiness, such that a violation of the rules in any particular instance becomes an offense to all, and so arouses everyone's desire to retaliate against the offender. Particular acts of stinginess do not fall into this category; they are not a fundamental threat to society's general interest of happiness, as a violation of justice. In other words, it is difficult to see how a perfect obligation to be charitable could evolve from the primitive instincts of self-defense and sympathy. Two questions emerge at this point: is stinginess morally wrong, and more generally, what other actions and/or omissions fall into this category of non-justice morality?

Exactly how to situate justice within the category of morality for Mill is a difficult question, in large part because he seems to make conflicting statements. To begin with, it will be necessary to understand Mill's formal definition of moral wrongness and rightness.

For the truth is, that the idea of penal sanction, which is the essence of law, enters not only into the conception of injustice, but into that of any kind of wrong. We do not call anything wrong, unless we mean to imply that a person ought to be punished in some way or other for doing it; if not by law, by the opinion of his fellow creatures; if not by opinion, by the reproaches of his own conscience . . . .we say that it would be right to do so and so, or merely that it would be desirable or laudable, according as we would wish to see the person whom it concerns, compelled, or only persuaded and exhorted, to act in that manner. (Mill 1969c, p. 246)

Moral judgment is the legitimate and hypothetical compelling of behavior, and it is easy to see how violating one of the rights of justice would arouse this judgment in all people. But Mill clearly states that imperfect obligations are also moral obligations, even though they do not generate any corresponding rights. Is it possible that Mill thinks that the violation of some moral obligations are punishable, but that others are not? It would appear not, as he unambiguously states that "It is part of the notion of Duty *in every one of its forms*, that a person may rightfully be compelled to fulfill it" (my italics). Moreover, he continues, "Duty is a thing which may be *exacted* from a person, as one exacts a debt" (Mill's italics) (Mill 1969c, p. 246). In light of these passages, it seems that stinginess is morally wrong, and hence punishable, despite not violating any rights. But this interpretation immediately runs into trouble. If stinginess is punishable, then it is not clear what other nonjustice moral violations are also punishable. In *On Liberty*, Mill states that everyone who enjoys the protections and benefits of society (i.e. everybody) is morally obligated to help contribute to the defense and maintenance of society, and that this obligation is "enforceable." Shortly thereafter, Mill states that only actions that violate rights are punishable. And so, if all moral obligations are enforceable, and their violations punishable—because a right has been violated—then Mill commits the very same error that he seeks to avoid, that of merging all of morality into justice (Mill 1977b, p. 279).

Various interpretations have been generated to address these issues, but unfortunately, they all require discounting certain passages, or creatively reconstructing Mill's conception of morality. For example, David Lyons considers moral wrongfulness to be the violation of a perfect moral obligation, whether it be of a moral right, or of a moral obligation. Justice entails respecting first order moral rights, whereas the remaining range of nonjustice morality consists of moral obligations, of which there are two categories. Fair-share burdens are those moral obligations (testifying in court, conscription, etc.) that apply to individuals who enjoy the many benefits of society; and individual beneficence, which might be required if someone is in dire need of our help (as in when one accidentally comes across someone who is drowning) (Lyons 1994, p. 140). Both types of moral obligations are enforceable because they are connected to second-order rights, or as Mill puts it in *On Liberty*, obligations that "by tacit understanding, ought to be considered as rights," but neither obligation is a demand of justice. Since no one has a right to our charity, our charity cannot be said to be fulfilling any kind of obligation of justice.

Moreover, because individuals have discretion as to when they are charitable, no single act of stinginess can be considered a violation of any moral obligation, and so cannot be considered morally wrong, in general. Mill is therefore not merging all of morality into justice, as violating the imperfect obligation of charity is not punishable. This interpretation, however, is only possible by "ignoring" Mill's distinction between morality and justice as being one between imperfect and perfect obligations, because for Lyons, the non-justice obligations of morality are still perfect obligations (Lyons 1994, p. 116). When Fred Berger considers these issues, he argues stinginess, being a violation of moral obligation, is morally wrong and punishable, and that there are no other obligations which are of the non-justice moral sort. Because Mill only discusses the imperfect obligation of charity, and Mill allows for discretion when fulfilling this obligation, there cannot be other non-justice obligations of morality. Like Lyons, Berger accepts that rights correspond to perfect obligations. Where they differ is that Berger reads Lyons' categories of non-justice moral obligations as being actually matters of justice. Enjoying the benefits of society may be understood as constituting a social contract, whereby individuals are perfectly obliged to perform their fair share of labor to maintain society. For the same reason, someone in distress might well have a right to help if a bystander were in a position to offer it, because anyone in that position should expect help. But even though all of these moral obligations are punishable, Berger differentiates between punishments for violations of perfect obligations, which can range from moral disapprobation to physical coercion, and punishments for violations of the imperfect obligation of charity, which can only be moral disapprobation. (Berger 1984, p. 224). Mill does conceive of punishment as ranging from one's guilty conscience to physical coercion, but nowhere in *Utilitarianism* does he distinguish between *kinds* of punishment.[6] On this account, Mill avoids merging all of morality into justice, because the violation of the imperfect obligation of charity is not punishable in the same way as violations of the perfect obligations of justice. However, Berger's interpretation is only possible by marginalizing the passage where Mill claims that *all* obligations can be extracted like a debt, or at least reading him to be referring only to obligations of justice, and not to the non-justice obligation of charity (Berger 1984, p. 225).

Morality vs expediency (and worthiness)

Both Lyons and Berger make plausible interpretations of the relationship between justice and morality, and there are others.[7] What is undeniable is that for Mill, morality is about duties and obligations that ultimately promote happiness, but morality does not demand the direct promotion of general happiness. Rather, it is a set of rules that *constrains* the maximization of general happiness. Morality establishes the minimum conditions for everyone to be able to pursue their own individual conceptions of happiness, which Mill implies will result in a greater share of overall happiness, than if morality demanded the direct maximization of it. In addition to the moral categories of wrong and right, there is a third category of actions that is neither prohibited nor obligatory. Mill does not discuss this category, which he calls 'Expediency or Worthiness', but he does briefly distinguish it from moral obligation.

> There are other things, on the contrary, which we wish that people should do, which we like or admire them for doing, perhaps dislike or despise them for not doing, but yet admit that they are not bound to do; it is not a case of moral obligation; we do not blame them, that is, we do not think that they are proper objects of punishment. (Mill 1969c, p. 246)

Considering that this passage is located in the middle of his articulation of wrongness and rightness, it is easy to think that Mill is here discussing imperfect obligations, but instead he is discussing a category of actions that is known as supererogatory—beneficent actions that go beyond the demands of moral obligation. Mill neglects this topic in *Utilitarianism*, which is understandable, considering that the chapter is about justice and not morality in general, but mapping this category out will clarify the relationship between justice, morality and expediency. Passages from *Auguste Comte and Positivism* provide much illumination.

> If in addition to fulfilling this obligation [of morality], persons make the good of others a direct object of disinterested exertions, postponing or sacrificing to it even innocent personal indulgences, they deserve gratitude and honour, and are fit objects of moral

praise. So long as they are in no way compelled to this conduct by any external pressure, there cannot be too much of it. (Mill 1969d, p. 337)

Mill is clearly describing the category of Expediency and Worthiness here, but his description reads much like how one would describe charity. If the beneficence of charity is obligatory and enforceable even in the mildest of forms, then Mill has still merged all of morality into justice. On the other hand, if charity is obligatory, and can be "extracted like a debt," but cannot be compelled, then Mill would seem to be confusing the imperfect obligation of charity with Expediency and Worthiness.

A third possible interpretation of the relationship between morality, charity, and supererogation comes from reviewing this discussion in *Auguste Comte and Positivism*. What neither Lyons nor Berger make clear in their interpretations is that a limited amount of charity is morally obligatory (and enforceable), and anything more is supererogatory. Without question, the preeminent obligations are those of justice. As Mill puts it, "It is incumbent on every one to restrain the pursuit of his personal objects within the limits consistent with the essential interests of others." Beyond that, "There is a standard of altruism to which all should be required to come up, and a degree beyond it which is not obligatory, but meritorious" (Mill 1969d, p. 337). The imperfect nature of the obligation of charity is established by the implicit contract that each citizen has with the rest of society.

And inasmuch as every one, who avails himself of the advantages of society, leads others to expect from him all such positive good offices and disinterested services as the moral improvement attained by mankind has rendered customary, he deserves moral blame if, without just cause, he disappoints that expectation. (Mill 1969d, p. 338)

A *limited* amount of charity is morally obligatory and enforceable only by moral disapprobation.[8] Mill thus avoids merging morality into justice. Everybody is not entitled to "all the good we can do them," but only a limited amount that has been established by custom (Mill 1969c, p. 247). As will be discussed in Chapter 5, there is a progressive dimension to Mill's thought. His principles and prescriptions must be understood as facilitating the improvement of individual character and society in general. He underscores this aspect of his thought by making clear that the scope of obligatory beneficence is to be ever expanding.

> Through this principle [of morality] the domain of moral duty, in an improving society, is always widening. When what once was uncommon virtue becomes common virtue, it comes to be numbered among obligations, while a degree exceeding what has grown common, remains simply meritorious. (Mill 1969d, p. 337)

Mill's formal definition of wrongness and rightness distinguish morality from Expediency or Worthiness, those actions we desire people to perform, but recognize that they under no obligation to do so. Because of the formality of his definition, there is no reason to suppose that Mill envisioned these categories to be fixed. This passage, as well as other writings, suggests the trajectory of moral improvement as customary beneficence expands, and the selfish desires become displaced by social ones. The end of this process, Mill calls the Religion of Humanity. It is when the general happiness is not only the standard of morality, but also a powerful object of desire in all individuals. It is not clear how large the imperfect obligation of beneficence becomes, but there are limits: Mill criticizes Comte and Calvinist ethics for categorizing all actions as either sin or duty. Highlighting the progressive distinction between the content of moral obligation and Worthiness makes clear how beneficence can be both obligatory and supererogatory.

One final point needs to be made regarding the distinction between morality and Expediency. Any attempt to establish a set of moral rules or rights, justified by the maximization of happiness or any other conception of utility, immediately faces the problem of what to do when violating a right would clearly promote happiness better than respecting it. Mill is aware of this possibility, and concedes that rights must yield in certain situations.

> [P]articular cases may occur in which some other social duty is so important, as to overrule any one of the general maxims of

justice. Thus, to save a life, it may not only be allowable, but a duty, to steal, or take by force, the necessary food or medicine, or to kidnap, and compel to officiate, the only qualified medical practitioner. In such cases, as we do not call anything justice which is not a virtue, we usually say, not that justice must give way to some other moral principle, but that what is just in ordinary cases is, by reason of that other principle, not just in the particular case. By this useful accommodation of language, the character of indefeasibility attributed to justice is kept up, and we are saved from the necessity of maintaining that there can be laudable injustice. (Mill 1969c, p. 259)

Circumstances are obviously a factor in morally appraising a situation. And rights are intended to identify rules so strict as to trump all other obligations or preferences. But if the strictness of the rule is based upon its essential contribution to the maximization of happiness, then the rule must yield when violating it would clearly promote more happiness than obedience to it. It must be remembered that according to the Art of Life, the rules that govern all practices, including conduct, are ultimately derived from, and justified by, one first principle.

the general principle to which all rules of practice ought to conform, and the test by which they should be tried, is that of conduciveness to the happiness of mankind . . . in other words, that the promotion of happiness is the ultimate principle of Teleology. (Mill 1974, p. 951)

Rights derive their legitimacy from their contribution to general happiness. So when circumstances are such that violating the right would promote more general happiness, then the right becomes invalid. In such circumstances, to paraphrase Mill, it is not that morality demands injustice, but that circumstances negate the right, thereby allowing that "other principle" to determine conduct in these rare instances. Although Mill does not name it, that other principle can only be the Principle of Utility.

This exception to perfect obligations of justice that Mill describes touches on a deeper problem for his conception of justice. If circumstances can sometimes require direct appeals to the Principle of Utility to settle conflicts between intermediary principles of conduct, then we may find that many of the obligations of justice, which Mill aims to preserve, are unjustifiable by the standard of general happiness. Despite Mill's arguments to the contrary, this criticism has persisted and has formed one of the central challenges of the traditional commentary on Mill. We will look more closely at this issue in Chapter 6.

CHAPTER FOUR

The Principle of Liberty
and its application

At the end of *A System of Logic*, Mill briefly discusses how his scientific method relates to the various practices in life. All practices fall into one of three departments, and *Utilitarianism* details the *summum bonum*, or ultimate standard, by which all departments are assessed. *Utilitarianism* also supplies Mill's formal definition of moral wrongfulness, which helps explain the evolution of the obligations of justice from the individual and primitive instinct to retaliate against threats to the interest of security, to the collective and moralized desire to punish threats to the interests of maintaining patterns of expected behavior. There remains to articulate the content of Mill's moral theory, and for this, one must turn to Mill's best known work, *On Liberty*. This essay is partly about the correct relationship between the state and the individual, but it is more about the correct relationship between individuals. It is about defining the actions that rightly arouse the desire to punish in others, and describing the beneficial consequences of each person refraining from those actions. At the same time, the essay is a critique of the prevailing social norms that wrongly lead people to want to punish certain harmless activities, which impedes the overall progress of society. *On Liberty* should be understood as articulating the social and legal principles that institute this progress. Mill is trying not only to change people's behavior, but also to change the way people think and feel about their behavior. To this end, Mill is focused on influencing the development of character. Hence, *On Liberty* should also be understood as a rough contribution to the abortive science of ethology, promised in *A System of Logic*. Much ink has been spilled grappling with *On Liberty*, and trying to fit it into Mill's larger doctrine. Its enduring attraction is partly to do with its ambiguities and internal tensions, but more to do to the fact that it addresses issues that are permanent and controversial in every pluralistic, liberal society.

The principle and expression

Mill's conception of progress placed European civilization at the very forefront of human development. This was not because of any inherent superiority, but because of the good fortune of its unique geographical and anthropological circumstances (Mill 1977a, p. 197). Europeans need to capitalize on these circumstances because the chief obstacles to progress have been largely of their own making. At the start of *On Liberty*, Mill surveys the history of the competition for political power to illustrate how it has often been used to halt progress in order for one group to maintain dominance over others. This competition was historically between self-appointed rulers and their people, but once democracy had firmly taken root, a fundamentally different type of power struggle ensued: in England, the chief obstacle to progress was now the democratic majority that exercised its power over the minority. Mill borrows the term "tyranny of the majority" from de Tocqueville's *Democracy in America* to describe the rise of this subtle, yet pervasive form of domination. Mill is particularly concerned about the dominance of the staid, middle class social norms of Victorian England that stifle critical thought and spirited discussion, which are the engines of intellectual and social progress. What makes this stage of the competition for political power fundamentally different than previous stages, is that the exercise of this power is not through physical or financial means, but by moral coercion.

> No one, indeed, acknowledges to himself that his standard of judgment is his own liking; but an opinion on a point of conduct, not supported by reasons, can only count as one person's preference; and if the reasons, when given, are a mere appeal

to a similar preference felt by other people, it is still only many people's liking instead of one. To an ordinary man, however, his own preference, thus supported, is not only a perfectly satisfactory reason, but the only one he generally has for any of his notions of morality, taste, or propriety, which are not expressly written in his religious creed; and his chief guide in the interpretation even of that. Men's opinions, accordingly, on what is laudable or blameable, are affected by all the multifarious causes which influence their wishes in regard to the conduct of others, and which are as numerous as those which determine their wishes on any other subject. (Mill 1977b, p. 221)

Individuals elevate their personal preferences about other people's conduct to the level of moral judgment, and apply them prejudicially to any deviation from the prevailing social norms. There is no standard or principle that guides people's moral appraisal, other than their own interests, or even worse, the interests of the upper class (which then influences how they interpret the moral obligations of their religion). This desire to punish deviations from social norms might seem to meet Mill's formal definition of moral wrongness, as provided in *Utilitarianism*, but the sentiment is not properly moral, because it serves only narrow interests, rather than the interests of general happiness. *On Liberty* is Mill's attempt to provide such a principle to govern people's moral appraisal of each other's conduct. His purpose is to protect the expression of individuality, which is the greatest source of individual happiness, and also a perpetual test of the expediency of prevailing social norms. At stake is not merely the liberty of eccentric individuals to parade around their nonconformity to Victorian culture, but the very forces of progress and innovation. Moreover, there is an insidiousness to the tyranny of majority that surpasses that of the abuse of power by the state.

Society can and does execute its own mandates: and if it issues wrong mandates instead of right, or any mandates at all in things with which it ought not to meddle, it practises a social tyranny more formidable than many kinds of political oppression, since, though not usually upheld by such extreme penalties, it leaves fewer means of escape, penetrating much more deeply into the details of life, and enslaving the soul itself. (Mill 1977b, p. 220)

Whereas the state might have some democratic or bureaucratic checks on the use of its power, social norms operate at the level of culture, which has a wider and deeper scope, and cannot be amended in a systematic way. Interestingly, Mill does not attempt to mitigate this influence; instead, he attempts to co-opt this influence, and direct it toward shaping individual character toward his ideal. His method is to define the terms under which individuals interact with each other, and with the state.

Mill's "one very simple principle," which is formulated in several different ways, is initially stated in general terms, and hints at its connection to justice: "that the sole end for which mankind are warranted, individually or collectively, in interfering with the liberty of action of any of their number, is self-protection" (Mill 1977b, p. 223). As described in *Utilitarianism*, justice has evolved over the generations as a system of protecting and maintaining society, and we are starting to see how Mill understands its moral obligations govern social conduct. In the very next sentence, Mill restates the Principle in more specific terms, "that the only purpose for which power can be rightly exercised over any member of a civilized community, against his will, is to prevent harm to others" (Mill 1977b, p. 223). This principle has come to be known as the Principle of Liberty; it states that individuals should be at complete liberty to do as they please, until their actions harm others without consent. If someone's action harms, or threatens to harm, another person, she then becomes eligible for society to coercively punish her, which can range from imprisonment, fines, moral approbation, or the guilt of her conscience. A person's own good provides no grounds for society or an individual to coercively interfere with the liberty of the person. Mill would seem to be describing the necessary and sufficient conditions for the use of coercion or punishment, but he clarifies that "it must by no means be supposed, because damage, or probability of damage, to the interests of others, can alone justify the interference of society, that therefore it always does justify such interference" (Mill 1977b, p. 292). Only harms that are a setback to essential interests justify punishment, and even then a utilitarian costs-benefits calculation is required to determine if the best punishment should be some form of legal punishment, the disapprobation of society, or if the internal sanctions of the offender's guilty conscience will suffice.

Mill immediately qualifies the Principle of Liberty by stating that it is only applicable to individuals who are in the "maturity of their faculties" (Mill 1977b, p. 224). Children, and by extrapolation, the mentally impaired, may rightly be coerced to protect them from themselves as well as from others. But once a person has reached the age of legal adulthood and full responsibility, it is not permissible to coerce or compel her to do what is thought to be best for her. Others may attempt to reason with her, or offer various incentives and disincentives to alter her behavior, but they cannot force her to do anything other than respect her moral obligations to others, which entails for the most part, not harming them. Similarly, "backward states" of people, or races in their "nonage" are also unprepared for the responsibilities of the Principle of Liberty (Ibid.). A people must be capable of spontaneous improvement before the Principle is the appropriate rule of social organization.

> Despotism is a legitimate mode of government in dealing with barbarians, provided the end be their improvement, and the means justified by actually effecting that end. Liberty, as a principle, has no application to any state of things anterior to the time when mankind have become capable of being improved by free and equal discussion. (Ibid.)

Mill thought these qualifications obvious. Liberty is not an end in itself, but the necessary means to his conception of human flourishing. As Mill clarifies when discussing applications of the Principle, those aspects of liberty that do not contribute to the goal of character development, or to utility in general, are not permitted. This conception of progress underpinning the argument for liberty will be discussed in the next two chapters. If a people are so desperate and selfish, and only capable of using liberty to forward their own narrow interests at the expense of others, then liberty is more of a dangerous liability than a condition of their progress. An authoritarian regime compelling deference to the law would be more beneficial, until a point is reached whereby each person's sympathy is expanded beyond their narrow kin-groups, and more interests are recognized, beyond their immediate physical and material needs. Even though the Principle of Liberty is based on forwarding the "permanent interests of man as a progressive being," these interests can not be tended to until a minimal level of security is established, and a critical level of intellectual development has been obtained (Ibid.).

The Principle of Liberty has the net effect of demarcating a realm wherein the individual is completely at liberty to do as she pleases. This self-regarding sphere is protected from not only legal and physical coercion but also from moral condemnation by the state or members of society, which Mill also considers a form of coercion. After establishing the Principle in the introduction, the next two chapters of the essay discuss two central liberties for Mill's project of individual and social reform: the liberty of thought and discussion, and the liberty of lifestyle. By allowing full scope for ideas to compete against each other, the liberty of thought and discussion is necessary both for individuals to consolidate the grounds of their own beliefs, and for the growth of knowledge in general. The obstacles to this freedom are largely external, so Mill considers three hypothetical cases of censorship to argue that it is never justified. The first case he considers is when the censored idea (or opinion, as Mill puts it) is true. When this type of censorship happens, people presume the truth of their own beliefs, and see nothing wrong with suppressing challenges to it. Censorship in this case, whether it be political or social, denies society a potentially valuable truth, which clearly impedes the promotion of utility. Moreover, Mill flatly rejects the argument that some ideas need to be protected from challenges because they are "useful," or have some utilitarian value, other than its truth. The judgment that an idea is useful is as fallible as the judgments of truth itself, and so provides no grounds for protecting the idea from critical challenges (Mill 1977b, p. 234). The second case Mill considers is when the censored idea is false. It may seem as though no harm is done by censoring a false idea, but Mill argues that false ideas are the only tools with which to test the truth of our own ideas. It is insufficient to simply hold the correct beliefs, one must also know the *grounds* of their beliefs and opinions, lest they become "dead dogma," instead of being maintained as a "living truth" (Mill 1977b, p. 243). So strongly does Mill consider the importance of conflicting ideas, that in the absence of any challenges to our established beliefs, it is incumbent on society to fabricate such challenges, as with a devil's advocate. The last hypothetical case of censorship that Mill considers is when the censored opinion contains a portion of the truth. This case is important, because Mill states that the vast majority of opinions contain only part of the truth. Again, Mill argues that the only way to separate the truth from the error of an opinion is to allow it to be freely discussed and debated. This last case reflects Mill's affinity for combining ideas from disparate thinkers like Bentham, Comte, and Coleridge, all of whose doctrines Mill thought contained only a portion of the truth. A free press had been established by the time Mill was writing *On Liberty*. Here Mill is more concerned with other forces in society exercising its informal sanctions to prevent the spreading of certain ideas, and the challenging of others.

Before discussing the distinction between self and others, we should note that Chapter II of the essay makes two claims the liberty of expression: one explicit, and the other implicit. The explicit claim is a sociological one regarding the growth of knowledge, namely, that knowledge can only grow in a society governed by the absolute liberty of thought and discussion. This aspect of Mill's argument for liberty bears the positivist influence of Auguste Comte, who thought that liberty was necessary for the growth of knowledge. For Comte, however, as truth becomes consolidated, the instrumental value of liberty is diminished and is eventually discarded altogether (Comte 1998, p. 61). For Mill, the value of liberty of thought and discussion is permanent, once a civilization becomes mature in their faculties. The implicit claim is a utilitarian one regarding the promotion of general happiness. Never explicitly stated in *On Liberty*, this claim is that growth of knowledge promotes happiness, and that the utilitarian benefits of free expression *always* outweigh its costs. It might have been easier to provide empirical evidence for Mill's argument in the nineteenth century, but recent historical experience casts doubt on the validity of this claim. Many countries that practice censorship and place little value on liberty have nonetheless advanced scientifically and culturally. There would seem to be no necessary connection between liberty and the growth of certain types of knowledge. This point will be discussed in more detail in the last chapter.

Self vs other-regarding conduct

The basis of all of Mill's thought is his conception of human nature, which he conceives as being fundamentally social in important respects. At the same time, in some other important respects, Mill thinks individuals are separate from each other. If all conduct was governed by the Principle of Liberty, a social and political space would be demarcated around each individual within which each would be free to live their lives any way they please. This self-regarding sphere is one of the key conditions to facilitating intellectual and social progress.

> It comprises, first, the inward domain of consciousness; demanding liberty of conscience, in the most comprehensive sense; liberty of thought and feeling; absolute freedom of opinion and sentiment on all subjects, practical or speculative, scientific, moral, or theological . . . Secondly, the principle requires liberty of tastes and pursuits; of framing the plan of our life to suit our own character; of doing as we like, subject to such consequences as may follow . . . Thirdly, from this liberty of each individual, follows the liberty, within the same limits, of combination among individuals; freedom to unite, for any purpose not involving harm to others. (Mill 1977b, p. 226)

The distinction between self and other regarding spheres is similar to the distinction between public and private realms, maintained by thinkers ranging from John Locke to John Rawls. For them, just as for Mill, the purpose of the distinction is to create realm where the rules of social conduct do not apply. Where they differ is exactly how the distinction between these realms are drawn. For Mill, the self-regarding sphere is slightly larger than the private realm is typically conceived, because it includes some public activities, specifically all activities that are harmless to others, such as sitting in the park reading a book or drinking a beverage. Even if the book was pornographic and the beverage alcoholic, the offense that the nearby prude and the teetotaler might experience would not be sufficient to render these actions other-regarding. In this respect, it is somewhat misleading to refer to it as the "self-regarding sphere," because some activities within this sphere will affect others, but in ways that are not relevant to the Principle. For example, Mill singles out the liberty of expression as involving other people, and so seemingly being governed by a different principle. But since it is so intimately linked to the liberty of thought, must be subsumed by the Principle of Liberty.[1] Mill considers some potential challenges to this distinction.

Drinking beer might itself be a self-regarding activity, but circumstances can quickly render this action other-regarding. For example, if one drinks excessively, one might be prevented from providing for others who are dependent on them, such as children. Or if by drinking, one is prevented from fulfilling some duty that one is contractually bound to perform, such as labor, then this may also render the simple act of drinking beer other-regarding. Finally, one may simply be setting a bad example to others by one's consumption of this intoxicating drink. Mill considers these seemingly self-regarding activities, and acknowledges that some actions normally considered self-regarding lose this status when others have legitimate claims on the actor. When the consumption of alcohol, or any otherwise self-regarding act, leads one to "violate a distinct and assignable obligation to any other person or persons," it is an other-regarding offense (Mill 1977b, p. 281). The drunkard who spends his days in the pub, rather than caring for his children, violates his legal and moral obligations. Similarly, a self-regarding action that prevents the performance of some "definite duty incumbent on him to the public" also becomes eligible for legal or social punishment. But Mill is only willing to go so far in accepting the consequences of some action on other people. Consequences that are merely "contingent," such as witnessing a bad example "neither violates any specific duty to the public, nor occasions perceptible hurt to any assignable individual," and so are tolerated by the Principle (Mill 1977b, p. 282). The drunkard who sits in his garden imbibing fine wine might be doing direct harm only to his own liver, but the causal link between the neighbor's kids witnessing him drink, and their own decision to start drinking is tenuous at best, because of all of the other intervening factors that go into their decision. Here, and in other places, Mill takes a somewhat conservative approach when making this distinction between actions that concern only the individual and actions that concern others. In order for an action to be considered other-regarding it must affect others "directly" and in "the first instance" (Mill 1977b, p. 225). For anything short of these immediate and perceptible effects on other people the individual cannot be held accountable.

The distinction is an important one: it would seem that without it, Mill's project never even gets off the ground. As one of *On Liberty*'s first critics, James Fitzjames Stephen, has argued, all actions affect others in some manner, so attempting to map out a self-regarding sphere within which individuals have full liberty is arbitrary. Stephen thought that humans were prone to vice, and so society needed to restrict the liberty of individuals to limit its spread (Stephen 1874, p. 151). Stephen is correct that any action can be described in such a way as to affect other people, but this need not be fatal to Mill's Principle. Rather than attempting to define the boundary between self and others by activity, as Mill initially does, a better strategy is to distinguish between categories of *effect* on others. All actions affect others in manners ranging from insignificant to significant, later in the essay, Mill switches his focus to isolating only those significant effects that are morally relevant to the Principle. Rather than focusing on *whether* an action affects others or not, he focuses on the *type* of effect on others, namely if the action produces harm. This move renders the debate over the strict boundary between the self and others insufficient, and consolidates the interpretive burden over Mill's conception of harm.

Harm and justice

In order to make Mill's Principle of Liberty realistic and applicable, we must concentrate on a narrow range of significant effects on people. Mill first cites self-defense as the only reason to interfere with the liberty of others, and his immediate restatement of the Principle specifies *harm* to others. An action must be judged to be harmful, or likely to be harmful, to another person before society or the law can consider coercing or punishing the actor. As will be discussed shortly, actions that harm only the actor himself are not eligible for coercion or interference. Much turns on the conception of harm with which Mill is working, and unfortunately, he does not provide a systematic account of it. If Mill is working with a very narrow conception of harm, for example, one that only includes physical or property damage, then the Principle of Liberty would be insufficient to protect against the various ways in which individuals can non-physically harm each other in a socially complex and interrelated society. In effect, the sphere of liberty would be too large, allowing psychological and political damage excluded from the narrow conception of harm. On the other hand, if Mill's conception of harm is broadly inclusive, then the Principle could lose its liberal character as it might be too restrictive, limiting the self-regarding sphere to trivial activities. Striking the correct balance with our interpretation of Mill's conception of harm will therefore be a crucial step in interpreting the Principle of Liberty. Once the conception of harm is established, we then see how it provides the substantive link between the obligations of justice, and the formal definition of wrongfulness.

It is important to keep in mind that Mill's purpose with articulating his principle was to protect individuals from the homogenizing and oppressive effects of Victorian society. The purpose was to protect and encourage the expression of individuality, which along with being the greatest source of happiness, also facilitates social progress. According to Mill, too many people were elevating their personal preferences about other people's conduct to the level of moral appraisal. English society was stagnating because novel and creative, harmless behavior was being morally condemned (Mill 1977b, p. 221). In order to provide a principle to govern when the desire to punish is properly moral, Mill differentiates between actions that are merely disliked or offensive, from actions that are truly harmful. *Only* harmful actions are eligible to be condemned as wrongful, and thus punishable. Despite not providing a systematic account of harm, he does, at various places, describe the effect that constitutes the necessary condition for the eligibility of punishment. He writes of "injuring the interests of" (Mill 1977b, p. 276), "damage, or probability of damage, to the interests of" (p. 292), and "actions as are prejudicial to the interests of" (p. 292) as the types of consequences that the Principle of Liberty is specifically aiming to prevent. Statements like these have led to the dominant interpretation in the literature that the conception of harm Mill uses relates to the notion of interests. By honing the conception of harm, it becomes possible to protect the actions of nonconformists and heretics, while establishing the conditions that must be met for legitimate moral condemnation and possibly coercive punishment.

This connection between harm and interests was first made by J. C. Rees (Rees 1996, p. 174). Rees points out that the early literature, which sought to differentiate between self and other-regarding actions, has conflated two very different scenarios that Mill describes at various points in *On Liberty*—actions that concerns others, and actions that affect their interests. Whereas Stephen is correct that any action can be described as affecting others, Mill's principle is only concerned with this significant type of affect—on others' interests. In light of the many times Mill refers to interests, this reading has good textual support, and is also the most plausible. The term "interest" refers to having a stake in the well-being of something (Feinberg 1984, p. 34). However, clarification is needed. For it can be said that a person may have an interest in her bodily integrity, just as much as in her favorite sports team, or even the protagonist in a gripping drama. Again, such an inclusive conception of harm would render the Principle of Liberty too constraining if the defeat of one's team, or any other trivial effect were to be included. The concept of interest must be refined in order to make it practical. Rees defers to "social recognition" and "prevailing standards" of behavior in society for his conception of interest, but this qualification still leaves too much latitude for a society to limit liberty with a broad conception of harm (Rees 1996, p. 175). Whereas most societies would acknowledge the interest one has in their bodily integrity, many would also consider heretical or blasphemous expressions injurious to other "socially recognized" interests. Such unpopular expressions are exactly the types of actions that Mill seeks to destigmatize. Dale Miller proposes interpreting Mill's conception of interest along the same lines as Rawls' primary goods (Miller 2010, p. 210). Such an account takes "interest" to refer to anything that is a means to executing a person's "rational plan of life," such as rights, liberties, opportunities, income and wealth (Rawls 1999, p. 54). Miller argues forcefully that this is a plausible interpretation of Mill's use of the concept, and I think *in practice*, these are the types of interests that Mill has in mind. But tying the concept of interests to individual life-plans would seem to render the concept more relativistic than Rees's interpretation. This, perhaps, is not surprising, because at the heart of Rawls' conception of justice is a commitment to neutrality between different conceptions of the good life; whereas for Mill, some forms of life, specifically those that privilege his character ideal, are inherently more valuable than others, by virtue of the amount of happiness they entail. This hierarchy of lifestyles suggest a slightly different conception of interests, one that is tied to justice and individuality.

In the previous chapter, I explained how justice, for mill, generates a system of rights. These [perfect] obligations of justice have evolved within human society from the interest of security protected by the primitive instincts of self-defense and sympathy. Despite the evolution and socialization of the notion of justice, there remains an animalistic aspect to it, because of the "extraordinarily important and impressive kind of utility which is concerned" with this interest.

The interest involved is that of security, to every one's feelings the most vital of all interests. Nearly all other earthly benefits are needed by one person, not needed by another; and many of them can, if necessary, be cheerfully forgone, or replaced by something else; no human being can possibly do without; on it we depend for all our immunity from evil, and for the whole value of all and every good, beyond the passing moment; since nothing but the gratification of the instant could be of any worth to us, if we could be deprived of everything the next instant by whoever was momentarily stronger than ourselves. (Mill 1969c, p. 251)

The interest of security is essential, and here Rawls would agree with Mill—whether one is neutral between conceptions of the good life, or prioritizes some over others, no human existence is possible without security. But is the right of security in one's body and property all Mill intends by interests? Perhaps at the earliest stages of human civilization. In Mill's discussion of justice, he describes how as humans came to recognize more essential and complex interests beyond their physical and material needs, and as they expanded the range of their sympathy beyond their immediate kin, patterns of expected behavior emerged that have shown to promote utility, such that deviations from them arouse the desire to punish the transgressor. And as successive generations came to rely on these patterns of expected behavior, they become enshrined as obligations of justice. Primitive humans had essential interests in their bodily security; now social humans also have essential interests in people deserving their treatment, contracts being honored, and impartiality and equality between individuals. People have different interests related to their individual goals, but all individuals share these essential interests, which warrant societal protection. To have a moral right is to have such a weighty interest that one can expect all of society to defend it (Mill 1969c, p. 250). *On Liberty* makes only veiled references to utilitarianism and only a tangential reference to justice. However, in one key passage, he does specify that the purpose of justice is to protect people's interests, and anyone living in society must limit their actions in certain ways.

[E]very one who receives the protection of society owes a return for the benefit, and the fact of living in society renders it indispensable that each should be bound to observe a certain line of conduct towards the rest. This conduct consists first, in not injuring the interests of one another; or rather certain interests, which, either by express legal provision or by tacit understanding, ought to be considered as rights; and secondly, in each person's bearing his share (to be fixed on some equitable principle) of the labours and sacrifices incurred for defending the society or its members from injury and molestation. (Mill 1977b, p. 276)

Now that we have a better understanding of the interests that are relevant to the Principle of Liberty, we can see how they delimit the realm of liberty Mill is attempting to define. Individuals are free to engage in whatever activities they wish, short of harming other's essential interests of justice. The system of rights defines the boundaries of liberty in any given society. To put it a different way, other people's rights define the boundaries of individuality in the self-regarding sphere of activity. Interpreted this way, the Principle of Liberty is not merely a negative principle of noninterference. It does require that individuals refrain from hurting each other or damaging their property. But behaving unequally or partially toward some particular person in public dealings might also constitute a violation of the discriminatee's rights. Or failing to fulfill an express or implied contract with someone would also constitute a harm, and be eligible for punishment according to the Principle. Moreover, the above passage specifies that all individuals who enjoy society's benefits are obligated to perform their share of the work necessary to maintain the society, such as serving on juries, fighting in the military, and offering assistance to any one in need. Mill derives this obligation from his contention that "A person may cause evil to others not only by his actions but by his inaction, and in either case he is justly accountable to them for the injury" (Mill 1977b, p. 225). Mill recognized the difficulty in protecting against harmful omissions, but concludes that because there are some "exceptional" cases, the possibility can be subsumed under the Principle of Liberty.

Several ambiguities arise from this interpretation that require clarification. For example, it is not clear whether the Principle of Liberty makes the prevention of harmful conduct the only reason for coercive interference, or if it aims to prevent harm in general. The former reading, first made by D. G. Brown, draws support from Mill's articulation of the Principle of Liberty as being directed toward the prevention of harm to others, as well as from other passages (Brown 1972, p. 135). It is quite a *Laissez faire* interpretation of the Principle, as it accepts the actual or potential harm to others as the only reason society can have for coercing people. In response, a second reading, made by David Lyons, draws support from Mill's initial articulation of the Principle as being concerned with societal self-protection, and from Mill's assertion that individuals in society can be compelled to help defend and maintain it (Lyons 1994, p. 93). It is a more expansive reading of the Principle, because it allows society to coerce individuals even when their conduct is harmless or self-regarding, in order to fulfill the positive obligations of maintaining society. Though the very liberal nature of Mill's doctrine might seem to hinge on this ambiguity, these two readings might not be so far apart. Brown and Lyons both accept that Mill requires all citizens to bear the burden of maintaining society (although they have different ways of connecting this obligation to the Principle of Liberty), and Mill casts this obligation in contractarian terms. And since Mill cautiously accepts that individuals can harm others by their acts of omissions, we can see how failing to bear one's share of the duties to maintain society does in fact harm others. The harm is that of disappointing reasonable exceptions, or breaking an express or implicit contract with all other citizens, and so the two readings are really not as far apart as might seem. How does the Principle of Liberty preclude the state from making overly burdensome demands of its citizens to prevent harm? As Miller points out, Mill only allows the state to make "equitable" demands on its citizens to maintain society, and given that the Principle of Liberty only supplies the necessary condition for legitimacy of coercion, a further utilitarian costs-benefits analysis must be employed before determining the most appropriate form of coercion (Miller 2010, p. 129). Another ambiguity is that the Principle of Liberty offers no guide to the appropriate amount of liberty that can be limited for the sake of security, or of any of the particular interests of justice. As will be discussed in Chapter 6, this is a serious gap in Mill's theory. We might respond that the Principle of Utility will make this determination, based on the facts of the situation, but appealing to the standard of general happiness is not possible without presupposing certain facts either about human nature, or about the trajectory of progress. Mill does consider these presumptions to be empirically supported, but a better characterization of this presupposition would be that it is a speculative extrapolation from his associationist psychology, or an "inductive wager" (Gray 1996, p.120). Even if we grant his presuppositions, it is not certain that the standard of general happiness would always tip in favor of liberty over security, as Mill assumes it would. More needs to be said on this point, and I will return to it in the last chapter of the book.

Individuality

The account of harm as setbacks to interests has wide acceptance in the secondary literature, despite there being some disagreement over which interests are relevant to the Principle of Liberty. Mill is clear, however, that the essential interests protected by justice are primary, as they are necessary for any project, especially human progress. Might there be other essential interests? Again, some interpretation is required. In *On Liberty*, Mill is primarily concerned with the oppressive and intolerant nature of Victorian social norms, but not because it necessarily threatens justice. Chapter III of the essay details how justice alone will not yield happiness.

> It is desirable, in short, that in things which do not primarily concern others, individuality should assert itself. Where, not the person's own character, but the traditions or customs of other people are the rule of conduct, there is wanting one of the principle ingredients of human happiness, and quite the chief ingredient of individual and social progress. (Mill 1977b, p. 261)

Here, Mill is describing the other essential interest of individuality—the freedom and desire to express one's unique qualities. Mill's valuation of individuality is one of the clearest expressions of the influence of German Romanticism on his revised utilitarianism. As one of the "principle" ingredients to happiness, it is clear that the purpose of the Principle of Liberty is to establish the social and political space-the self-regarding sphere-within which individuality is expressed. Unfortunately, the connections to *Utilitarianism* are obscure, thereby requiring some interpretation to reconstruct his argument. But in the introduction to *On Liberty*, Mill makes clear that the Principle of Liberty is justified because of its contribution to utility.

It is proper to state that I forgo any advantage which could be derived to my argument from the idea of abstract right, as a thing independent of utility. I regard utility as the ultimate appeal on all ethical questions; but it must be utility in the largest sense, grounded on the permanent interests of man as a progressive being. (Mill 1977b, p. 224)

This passage is the crucial because it affirms Mills' commitment to utilitarianism, states that humans have permanent interests, and describes human nature as fundamentally progressive. The Principle of Liberty is not simply about narrow expediency, but is about maintaining the necessary conditions for individuals to develop their own characters, which in turn stimulates progress toward a greater stock of general happiness. As I discussed in Chapter 2, understanding the formation of character for Mill is the key to reforming society. So broad is the scope of Mill's reforms that they entail changing behavior, and the way one feels about one's behavior. In Chapter 3, we saw that these reforms should be oriented around developing the mental capacities to experience the higher pleasures. In *On Liberty*, we learn that these faculties are exercised by expressing individuality.

We must be clear about the essential interest of individuality, and how it is impeded by oppressive social norms. Victorian society limited individual choice in every department of life. In some cases, the power of tradition and custom was so strong as to eliminate choosing altogether. Mill is not advocating dispensing with hundreds of years of experience embodied in tradition, because he recognized that it makes much information available to the current generation. The key for each individual is "to find out what part of recorded experience is properly applicable to his own circumstance and character" (Mill 1977b, p. 262). The problem with Victorian society is that it imposed tradition and custom to such an extent, it denied people the exercise of their distinctly human capacity of choice-making.

The human faculties of perception, judgment, discriminative feeling, mental activity, and even moral preference, are exercised only in making a choice. He who does anything because it is the custom, makes no choice. He gains no practice either in discerning or in desiring what is best. The mental and moral, like the muscular powers, are improved only by being used. (Mill 1977b, p. 262)

These faculties comprise the capacity to experience the higher pleasures. Mill does not explicitly name individuality as a higher pleasure, but as a "principle" ingredient to happiness that utilizes "human faculties," it could not be anything else. For Mill, the capacity to experience the higher pleasures is one of the distinguishing features of the human species. Although these capacities are generic, they must be actively cultivated. And like the capacity to experience higher pleasures, the faculties that enable individuality can easily atrophy and wither from lack of exercise. The harm of an oppressive and homogenizing culture is that it impedes the exercise of these capacities, and ultimately the expression of individuality.

The centrality of choice-making to express individuality has led some scholars to interpret Mill as employing a conception of autonomy.[2] Mill never uses the term, but his discussion of individuality does resemble this contemporary concept. Some have even gone so far as to ascribe autonomy as a "vital interest," superior to security. (Gray 1996, p. 52). I prefer not to try to foist this concept onto Mill's thought, as I believe it confuses the issue. The contemporary conception of autonomy usually entails rational and critically reflective choice-making, combined with an independence from external influences on the choice. The defining aspect of this conception of choice-making is the fact that it is purely procedural. That is to say, the value of autonomously choosing is derived less from the choice, and more from the rational process used to make the choice. Mill certainly values rational deliberation, and *On Liberty* is a testament to his commitment to the independence of the choice-making conditions, but the *choice* one makes is also as important for Mill. If one were to develop the capacity to appreciate the higher pleasures, but after some experimentation decided to commit to a life rich in many lower pleasures, then Mill would reject the choice as being the product of faulty reasoning. It is an empirical fact for Mill that humans always prefer the higher pleasures over lower ones, all things being equal. It might be possible to identify a purely procedural conception of autonomy, but it would be subordinate to the substantive demands of individuality (the correct choice), and so adds little to our understanding of this essential interest.

The harm that oppressive social norms do to individuals is only partly due to it impeding the human faculties involved in choice-making. The interest of individuality is largely derived from actually finding a lifestyle that conforms to one's unique dispositions, or "internal culture" (Mill 1981, p. 147). A life that is not an expression of these dispositions is not individual, even if it was chosen under ideal choice-making conditions. As Mill puts it, "his own mode of laying out his existence is the best, not because it is the best in itself, but because it is his own mode." Humans possess generic faculties of mind (in varying degrees of strength), but there are also important differences between individuals.

> Human beings are not like sheep; and even sheep are not undistinguishably alike. A man cannot get a coat or a pair of boots to fit him, unless they are either made to his measure, or he has a whole warehouseful to choose from: and is it easier to fit him with a life than with a coat, or are human beings more like one another in their whole physical and spiritual conformation than in the shape of their feet? If it were only that people have diversities of taste, that is reason enough for not attempting to shape them all after one model. But different persons also require different conditions for their spiritual development . . . (Mill 1977b, p. 270)

Mill is not positing a discrete essence that requires to be expressed in some definite practice or lifestyle. But individuals do need to be authentic about their desires, and honest about how they evaluate their lives. There is the element of discovery to individuality, and the ultimate standards of this interest are internal. If the fallibility of human knowledge requires the liberty of thought and discussion to promote the growth of knowledge, then there is a greater uncertainty about the forms of life that entail individual flourishing. Human flourishing necessarily entails the higher pleasures, but there are indefinite ways for it to do so. Individuality requires that people are capable to perform "experiments of living" in order to develop their unique dispositions and talents in a way that best satisfies the demands of one's unique qualities.

> Human nature is not a machine to be built after a model, and set to do exactly the work prescribed for it, but a tree, which requires to grow and develop itself on all sides, according to the tendency of inward forces which make it a living thing. (Mill 1977b, p. 263)

This Romantic conception of human nature, and the necessity for freedom for its flourishing, is heavily influenced by the German thinker, Wilhelm von Humbodlt. Humboldt is the only thinker Mill praises repeatedly in *On Liberty*, and even begins the essay with an epigraph from Humboldt's work, the *Limits of State Action*. Hailing from a completely different tradition than British Empiricism, Humboldt's influence forms a core aspect of Mill's doctrine of reform. Human nature is fundamentally social, but reason demands that the true end for each individual is "the highest and most harmonious development of his powers to a complete and consistent whole" (Humboldt 1993, p. 10). The conflicting demands of community and individual liberty are reconciled in the concept of *bildung*: the "fullest, richest, and most harmonious development of the potentialities of the individual, the community, or the human race" (Burrow 1994, p. xxix). For Humboldt, the paternalistic and bureaucratic state is the primary obstacle to his vision of self-realization. Mill also advocates for a limited state, but is primarily concerned with the "despotism of custom" exercised by Victorian social norms and their defenders as the primary obstacle to individuality.

What then, is the moral status of individuality? As an essential interest, along with justice, it is ranked above other disparate interests in the success of people's lives. But there is no independent *right to individuality*. Individuality is protected primarily by the rights that protect justice. If all people respect each other's rights, including refraining from inappropriately morally condemning each other for harmless deviations from the dominant social norms, then individuality will be largely protected, or at least the conditions for it. The manner in which I have been characterizing the interest of individuality might suggest that it is an solitary endeavor, but this would be mistake. As Mill puts it, "It would be a great misunderstanding of this doctrine to suppose that it is one of selfish indifference" (Mill 1977b, p. 276). The development of individuality is very much a social project, and other people are morally obliged to assist. In *Utilitarianism*, Mill describes the category of non-justice moral obligations, and cites only charity as an example of this obligation. Elsewhere, he describes "a standard of altruism to which all should be required to come up" (Mill 1969d, p. 337). In *On Liberty*, Mill articulates what some of these moral obligations entail—individuals are required to help each other develop their individualities.

Human beings owe to each other help to distinguish the better from the worse, and encouragement to choose the former and avoid the latter. They should be forever stimulating each other to increased exercise of their higher faculties, and increased direction of their feelings and aims toward wise instead of foolish, elevating instead of degrading, objects and contemplations. (Mill 1977b, p. 277)

This moral obligation requires individuals to positively help others in their efforts to develop their faculties. At the same time, the Principle of Liberty forbids coercive interference with their liberty, even if to help them. The crucial distinction then is between those forms of influence that are coercive, and those that are non-coercive, or rather what constitutes "encouragement." This obligation makes clear the deeply social, and almost communitarian, nature of individual flourishing for Mill, but it also highlights the important fact that Mill is trying to strike the right balance between individual liberty and social influence.

Penalties vs punishments

Without question, Mill places liberty at the heart of his social doctrine, but its centrality has overshadowed the social influence individuals are rightly to experience in the course of developing their characters. Defying dominant social norms takes personal strength, and developing the capacities to appreciate the higher pleasures often entails discontent. For Mill, developing the strength of character necessary to resist prescribed forms of life, and to develop the faculties of the mind is, in part, a social endeavor. In particular, social elites, that is, individuals who have already developed Mill's ideal character type, would be the primary agents directing the social influence, by serving as models of reform (Mill 1977b, p. 269). The key to this ethological strategy is to differentiate between the punishments individuals would experience for their violations of moral obligation (e.g. harming other people), and the "natural penalties" that individuals would experience as a consequence of their lowly characters. The success of Mill's entire project—that of encouraging certain character traits and discouraging others, all within the parameters of the Principle of Liberty—hinges on the success of this distinction.

The primary virtue Mill extols is that of an energetic character with strong impulses. An abundance of energy can be channeled in anti-social ways, "but more good may always be made of an energetic nature, than of an indolent or impassive one" (Mill 1977b, p. 263). In *Considerations on Representative Government*, Mill points out that, "it is much easier for an active mind to acquire the virtues of patience, than for a passive one to assume those of energy" (Mill 1977c, p. 407). However, such energy needs to be brought under control and balanced with discipline: "Pagan self-assertion" needs to be combined with "Christian Self-denial" (Mill 1977b, p. 266). At the same time, it is not sufficient to have disciplined energy, for it must also be *one's own*. "One whose desires and impulses are not his own, has no character, no more than a steam engine has a character" (Mill 1977b, p. 264). To allow custom and the will of others to determine one's impulses is to allow these faculties to atrophy, and therefore to deny oneself an important source of happiness. The key to making one's impulses an expression of their individuality is to exercise the generic human faculties involved in choice-making. Some people may naturally possess the strength of character to develop these faculties in the face of the despotism of custom, but in Chapter IV of *On Liberty*, Mill describes the development of this character type to be largely the product of social influence. However one develops this character, they are then morally obliged (up to a point) to help others reform theirs.

> The is always need of persons not only to discover new truths, and point out when what were once truths are true no longer, but also to commence new practices, and set an example of more enlightened conduct, and better taste and sense in human life. (Mill 1977b, p. 267)

Progress is lead and motivated by persons of strong character. Such people have conducted their own experiments in living and have discovered new practices that improve upon out-dated ones. They display high levels of individuality, and so are also the "competent judges", referenced in *Utilitarianism*, and capable of identifying higher pleasures. The ultimate goal of Mill's reforms, spanning across his writings is this: however one chooses to pursue the higher pleasures and express their individuality, they will need to develop this character ideal, because internal and external forces are working against this goal.

Despite Mill describing the progressive nature of human civilization, he recognized that there is also an opposite trend toward mediocrity and conformity to tradition (Mill 1977b, p. 268). As the despotism of custom taxes an individual's strength of character, she becomes less capable of resisting the worst desires and tendencies of her character. Just as Mill is clear about the character traits that embody individual flourishing, he is equally clear about the lowly character types that are its chief obstacles.

> A person who shows rashness, obstinacy, self-conceit – who cannot live within modest means – who cannot restrain himself from hurtful indulgences – who pursues the animal pleasures at the expense of those of feeling and intellect – must expect to be lowered in the opinion of others, and to have a less share of their favorable sentiments. (Mill 1977b, p. 278)

These character flaws, it should be made clear, are all harmless to others. As qualities of an individual, as opposed to actions of the individual, these traits would seem to have no relevance to the Principle of Liberty. And yet, Mill states that:

> There is a degree of folly, and a degree of what may be called (though the phrase is not unobjectionable) lowness or deprivation of taste, which, though it cannot justify doing harm to the person who manifests it, renders him necessarily and properly a subject of distaste, or, in extreme cases, even of contempt (Mill 1977b, p. 278)

These lowly traits do not inspire in others the desire to punish, but they do elicit a highly critical response from others. Such consequences are the decisions that fully developed elites make about how they conduct their affairs, as aspects of their individuality.

> We are not bound, for example, to seek his society; we have a right to avoid it (though not to parade the avoidance), for we have a right to choose the society most acceptable to us. We have a right, and it may be our duty, to caution others against him, if we think his example or conversation likely to have a pernicious

effect on those with whom he associates. We may give others a preference over him in optional good offices, except those which tend to his improvement. (Mill 1977b, p. 278)

Such tolerant disapproval serves to alter the incentive structure of lowly behavior: if individuals bear the full cost of their defective characters, they might be compelled to reform them. The Principle of Liberty expressly forbids coercing someone for their good, and so the consequences, or disincentives, Mill prescribes are not the punishments applicable for violations of moral obligation. They are nonetheless significant.

> In these various modes a person may suffer very severe penalties at the hands of others, for faults which directly concern only himself; but he suffers these penalties only in so far as they are the natural, and, as it were, the spontaneous consequences of the faults themselves, not because they are purposely inflicted on him for the sake of punishment. (Ibid.)

Mill stresses that the nature of these consequences are categorically different than the consequences for violating moral obligation, although possibly as severe. The penalties are the natural and spontaneous consequences of, and inseparable from, lowly behavior. What is important about these passages is Mill's *endorsement* of these reactions to individuals who display these lowly traits. He is not lamenting the unfortunate consequences that some people will experience as they squander their lives, harming no one but themselves; he is employing them.

The challenge for Mill's project of reform is to maintain two very different responses for two different kinds of offenses. He stresses that the distinction between "the loss of consideration which a person may rightly incur" for lowly behavior, and the "reprobation which is due him" for violating moral obligation "makes a vast difference both in our feelings and in our conduct toward him" (Mill 1977b, p. 279). For behavior lowly and undignified, society penalizes the individual in the form of ostracism and contempt; for behavior harmful to others, society must punish the individual in the form of legal, social, or, moral coercion. However, the passages above make clear that Mill focuses primarily on the *reasons* for each type of interferences, and less on the *effects*. Considered from the individual's point of view, a particular penalty may not be coercive in itself, but the aggregate of society's penalties might constitute coercive influence. If in practice the severe penalties consequent of lowly behavior are no different than the punishment that results from violations of moral obligations, then Mill will have made no progress over the despotism of custom he attacks. The Principle of Liberty would provide no protection for an individual attempting to resist the prevailing social norms, and express her individuality. This potential contradiction of the Principle of Liberty has contributed to some marginal interpretations of Mill's project, some of which attribute wholly illiberal intentions.[3] Such interpretations are unsustainable, and have been forcefully refuted, but are nonetheless correct in identifying high levels of social influence allowed by the Principle.[4] In order to understand how individual liberty is protected, despite the influence rightly exercised by society, we must consider that at the outset of the essay, Mill prefaces that his argument only concerns "Social Liberty," and not the "liberty of the Will" (Mill 1977b, p. 217). In other words, the Principle is not concerned with the origins of one's desires, only one's ability to satisfy them. This narrow focus on negative liberty enables individuals to exercise and act on their human faculties of choice, and also allows for social elites to influence that faculty, up to a point (Kumar 2010). Mill draws the line at moral coercion: society may alter the incentive structures surrounding all sorts of behavior by encouragement, avoidance, or ostracism, but it cannot morally condemn lowly behavior unless a moral obligation has been broken. So from the individual's point of view, she may *feel* as though the sum total of her peers' penalties are leaving her with little choice in some matter, provided she actually does have a choice (by which I mean her peers are not physically, financially, or morally compelling her), then she is free as far as the Principle of Liberty is concerned. This reading of the Principle of Liberty will not satisfy those who regard influences on the rational choice-making process as forms of coercion or impositions on freedom, but their legitimate concerns are discussed in *A System of Logic*, where Mill discusses determinism (Mill 1974, p. 836). In *On Liberty*, Mill largely steers clear of the normative issues surrounding the formation of one's desires, and instead accepts that there will be diverse influences on the formation of a person's will.

Before moving on to look at applications of the Principle of Liberty, one last clarification must be made regarding the influence of society. Mill is concerned to articulate the legitimate forms of influence that society can exercise over the individual because he is aware that there are two independent forces in society trying to influence people's behavior: those that suppress nonconformity and individuality, in an effort to defend the dominant social norms, and those that disincentivize lowly behavior in order to facilitate character reform. Chapter III of *On Liberty* discusses how the Principle of Liberty helps protect against the former influence; whereas Chapter IV discusses how the Principle allows the latter form of influence (Kumar 2006, p. 142). Provided society—whether the retrograde defenders of Victorian social norms, or the developed social elites—do not coerce the individual, they may respond to an individual's behavior and character any way they please. To be clear, the Principle does not privilege the efforts of the social elites over those of the defenders of Victorian social norms. Other institutions and values in society might do so, but the Principle itself allows for individuals and society to evolve (or devolve) in various ways. I think it is fair to say that lurking just below the surface of the text is the presumption that the influence of the developed elites would prevail over the defenders of Victorianism. Mill did see human society improving in important ways, but progress could be impeded indefinitely.

Some applications

In the last chapter of *On Liberty*, Mill discusses some applications of his Principle of Liberty. Some of these applications illuminate and clarify how he intends the Principle to apply to some tricky cases, and others seem to contradict Mill's entire program in the Essay. Space precludes a detailed survey of all of these applications, so I will limit myself to three that I think illustrate something important about the Principle. First, I will discuss how the Principle operates in the free market, because this illustrates how the Principle is only justifiable insofar as it promotes utility. Where some other principle is expedient, the Principle of Liberty yields. Next, I will look at Mill's perplexing exclusion from the self-regarding sphere, actions that offend standards of common decency. This "obvious limitation" to the Principle would seem to cede all of the resources necessary to the defenders of Victorian social norms; it will therefore have to be explained, or dismissed. Last, I will discuss Mill's views on the family, and how he feels that too much liberty is granted to parents with regard to the treatment of their children. Mill makes some claims that seem shockingly illiberal from the contemporary perspective, but I will show how these claims really illustrate Mill's commitment to the progressive interests of Mankind.

The free market

The first statement of the Principle of Liberty gives the impression that every case of harm to others justifies punishment, but as we integrate Mill's formal conception of morality from *Utilitarianism*, we see that only wrongful harms warrant punishment, and even then, some harms are calculated not to be worth punishing by the coercive apparatus of the state. The very first case that Mill discusses in the chapter is competition in the free market. He recognized that as the Principle has been presented, failure in the market would seem to meet the necessary and sufficient conditions to warrant protection by the Principle of Liberty.

> Whoever succeeds in an overcrowded profession, or in a competitive examination; whoever is preferred to another in any contest for an object which both desire, reaps the benefit from the loss of others, from their wasted exertion and their disappointment. But it is, by common admission, better for the general interest of mankind, that persons should pursue their objects undeterred by this sort of consequences. In other words, society admits no right, either legal or moral, in the disappointed competitors, to immunity from this kind of suffering. (Mill 1977b, p. 292)

Mill is acknowledging that failure in a competitive market is a harm caused directly by the actions of other people. The reason that it is not a punishable action is because society has recognized no such right. As the primitive, individual notion of security evolves into the social system of justice, protection against this type of harm proves not to contribute to general happiness: "it is now recognized . . . that both the cheapness and good quality of commodities are most effectually provided for by leaving the producers and sellers perfectly free, under the sole check of equal freedom to the buyers for supplying themselves elsewhere" (Mill 1977b, p. 293). This admitted exception to the Principle of Liberty is called the Doctrine of Free Trade, or the Laissez Faire Principle, and he discusses it at length in *Principles of Political Economy* (Mill 1965, p. 936). The Doctrine does not prohibit all restrictions on the free market, because some restrictions are expedient, such as laws against deception, or minimal health and safety standards. It is worth reminding that the Principle of Liberty's ultimate justification is that it contributes to general happiness. Where it fails to do so, some other principle must step in to contribute to this ultimate end. This other principle, the Doctrine of Free Trade, is equally limited only insofar as it promotes general happiness. Some aspects of the free market might be legitimately regulated, such as the sale of poisons. Poisons, and by extension firearms, are often used to wrongfully harm others. If this were their only uses, then Mill says it would be legitimate to prohibit their production and sale. But since there are "innocent" uses for such dangerous products, it is only appropriate to regulate them (Mill 1977b, p. 294).

A more difficult aspect of the free market is solicitation—the attempts to induce someone to engage in some activity they might not otherwise. The consumption of drugs, the purchasing of sex, or gambling are all permitted by the Principle of Liberty, except when these acts directly lead one to violate a moral obligation. Since these acts are otherwise permitted, it must also be permitted to advice to perform these acts. But, solicitation, being a form of expression, is not strictly a self-regarding action. The difficulty sets in when the person doing the advising is also someone who profits from the act. The question of solicitation of harmful actions is not one of either liberty or prohibition; Mill casts the two sides of the debate as being between consistency and falliblism. On the one hand, Mill recognized that if the state accepts the liberty of individuals to engage in some self-regarding activity, then it would be contradictory to criminalize the labor of people who cater to that activity. The state should either allow the activity and its derivative industry, or prohibit both (Mill 1977b, p. 296). On the other hand, even though the state cannot compel one to do what is in that person's self-regarding interest to do, it may still deem some actions to be harmful or undignified. But when the state or anyone, makes such a judgment about what is in a person's interests, it does so fallibly. It would be therefore legitimate then for the state to limit the actions and expressions of partial and financially interested facilitators of the harmful activity to influence the decision of each person. Mill does not definitively come down on one side or the other, but he seems more inclined toward the latter argument (Mill 1977b, p. 297). In practice, this would mean that prostitution, for example, would be legal in people's homes, or in private clubs, but that prostitutes would not be able to solicit in public places. Some countries, such as the United Kingdom, have adopted such policies with regard to gambling, but a more common example of this reasoning can be found in the ban on advertising cigarettes and liquor in many countries.

Indecency

As we have discussed, one of the obligations of people living in an organized society is to help maintain it and defend against harms, even if that requires physically stopping someone from crossing a dangerous bridge, when there is no time to warn them. (If, after being fully informed of the risk of crossing the bridge, the pedestrian still chooses to do so, then there can be no interference with his dangerous crossing.) Similarly, Mill cautiously grants that the state may take preventative measures to prevent harms to society, even if they interfere with the liberty of its members, such as prohibiting a person from drinking if they are prone to violence when drunk. Or, it would be permissible for the state to punish someone for idleness, if they were receiving some form of public support. These "obvious limitations" to the Principle of Liberty are fairly straightforward when we see that circumstance render these actions, other-regarding. However, in the paragraph that immediately follows this discussion, there is a passage that proves very difficult to integrate into Mill's doctrine.

> Again, there are many acts, which, being directly injurious only to the agents themselves, ought not to be interdicted, but which, if done publicly, are a violation of good manners, and coming thus within the category of offences against others, may rightly be prohibited. Of this kind are offences against decency; on which it is unnecessary to dwell, the rather as they are only connected indirectly with our subject, the objection to publicity being equally strong in the case of many actions not in themselves condemnable, nor supposed to be so. (Mill 1977b, p. 295)

The key aspect of this offense is its publicity. The same act, if performed in private would not be punishable. It is not clear if the passage is a continuation of his discussion of the "obvious limitations" to the Principle, or if a public violation of "good manners" constitutes a harm to others. Either way, the passage seems to subvert the whole thrust of the argument for liberty, by giving the defenders of the Victorian social norms all the resources they need to coercively impose their way of life upon everyone. The passage also seems to contradict other passages that deal with similar issues. For example, he states that even within a country whose majority was Muslim, it would be wrong to prohibit the consumption of pork, despite the widespread offense caused[5] (Mill 1977b, p. 285). This position is the one that naturally fits with the Principle of Liberty, that mere dislike or offense does not rise to the status of harm, and must therefore be tolerated by society, in the interest of allowing individuals to live their own unique lives. Unfortunately, the passage is clear about the punishability of indecency and violations of good manners, and Mill quickly moves onto the next topic without any clarification of this case.

Efforts to incorporate this passage into the Mill argument have been fruitless. Johnathan Wolfe concludes that either Mill was aware that this "Indecency Principle" was a contradiction of the Principle of Liberty, or that the concept of harm that Mill is using is so broad as to include public offenses against good manners (Wolfe 1998, p. 15). At the risk of being uncharitable to Mill, I think the best explanation is that he did see good manners and public decency as limitations to the Principle. In other words, Mill recognized that indecency and violations of good manners are not harms in the relevant sense, but he is nonetheless willing to enforce such cultural mores. Like the previous two "obvious limitations" he discusses, Mill considers indecency a special case that would not limit a significant portion of liberty. How many violent alcoholics could there really be in society? Mill presumes—perhaps naively— very few. Similarly, Mill presumes that very few expressions of individuality would be indecent, and he would probably endorse the ensuing penalties and punishments for those that were. Scholars and contemporary admirers of Mill should never forget that despite how progressive his principles are, he was still very much a product of the Victorian culture that he attacked. From his views about races in their "nonage" to his preference that women prioritize their domestic duties, some of Mill's views very much reflect the prejudices and presumptions of his time. The standards of decency then were probably far less contentious in Mill's time than today, and so he did conceive that they could be used as tools oppression. The entire essay is about the benefits of liberty; because Mill thought this issue was only "indirectly" connected to the argument of the essay, we can infer that the liberty to be indecent and violate good manners do not seem relevant to his conception of individuality. The frustratingly brief manner in which he deals with the topic attests to his view that this limit to the freedom of expression really is obvious.

The liberty of parents

The last case we will examine is one of misplaced liberty. Liberty is often denied to people in certain areas of life, but it can also be wrongly granted to people in other areas. In the family, for example, husbands are given total liberty to conduct the affairs of their entire family as if they were entirely his own. The "almost despotic power" that husbands exercise over their wives is a case where Mill argues the state should be more vigilant of wrongful harms to its citizens. This protection need not entail an expansion of state power: simply granting the same rights to women (especially property and divorce rights) as to men would go a very long way in empowering wives, and equalizing relationships within the family. Despite the family being the one of the largest contributors to general happiness, Mill does not dwell on this topic because the defenders of this form of oppression do not invoke liberty as their defense (Mill 1977b, p. 301). One case where husbands do claim liberty is with regard to the care of their children. All people recognize the "sacred" duty of parents to educate their children, and yet society is unwilling to hold parents legally responsible for this obligation.

> It still remains unrecognised, that to bring a child into existence without a fair prospect of being able, not only to provide food for its body, but instruction and training for its mind, is a moral crime, both against the unfortunate offspring and against society

and that if the parent does not fulfill this obligation, the State ought to see it fulfilled, at the charge, as far as possible, of the parent. (Mill 1977b, p. 302)

That Mill considers the neglect of education a "moral crime," means that for Mill it is a definite harm to the child, and so not a question of liberty. The fact that it should be enforced by law, beyond opinion, means that the utilitarian benefits outweigh the costs of this level of enforcement. Rather than provide education at state-run schools (which the English state did in Mill's time), the state should require education, but then provide financial assistance to lower income families to cover the costs. This arrangement would leave the choice of instruction the prerogative of the parents, while guaranteeing some minimal level of education, as tested by state-run exams. Mill laments the fact that there is not even a public sentiment willing to enforce this sacred duty of properly educating one's children.

The duty to educate one's child is part of the larger obligation of all married couples: to only have children if they possess the resources to properly care for them. A couple's decision to have a child or not might seem to be a paradigmatic example of a self-regarding choice, but procreating is an other-regarding act that warrants societal or state regulation for three reasons. First, the act of bringing a child into the world creates another person whose distinct interests must be considered when assessing whether the actions of the parents are self or other regarding. Even though the Principle of Liberty does not apply to children below the age maturity, does not mean that they have no moral rights. Abusing one's child is certainly a moral crime, and is also a legal crime in many countries. Second, the act of giving birth can also be said to establish a contractual agreement between the parents and the child. The child receives sufficient care in exchange for obedience, and, in some working and middle class families, labor. Third, bringing a new life into existence poses risks not only to the child, but also to society. Mill claims it is a crime not to provide at least the "ordinary chances" for a normal life to a child (Mill 1977b, p. 304). The child, and her future contribution to society, also poses risks to the labor market.

And in a country either over-peopled, or threatened with being so, to produce children, beyond a very small number, with the effect of reducing the reward of labour by their competition, is a serious offence against all who live by the remuneration of their labour. (Mill 1977b, p. 304)

Mill was deeply influenced by the Malthusian concern for over-population. This concern leads Mill to posit a causal connection between population and the overall welfare of society (Mill 1965, p. 154). For Malthus, as for Mill, the relative growth in population does not correspond to a relative grown in prosperity of society, because the additional labor would not produce sufficient resources to sustain the larger population. The increased number of laborers also drives the costs of labor down because of the increased supply of it. In fact, a large contributor to the conditions of the working classes was the large number of dependents on a single paycheck (Mill 1965, p. 351). Mill therefore approves of those laws in some European countries that require a couple to provide evidence of their financial self-sufficiency before granting a marriage license. This law would be difficult to enforce, so where law enforcement is not expedient, there should be at least the moral disapprobation of society.

These cases of misapplied notions of liberty highlight an important dimension to Mill's conception of morally relevant harm. By specifying "definite damage," or "perceptible hurt," and excluding "merely contingent" harms, or "constructive injury" as being relevant to the Principle of Liberty, Mill suggests a narrow reading of the necessary condition for the appropriateness of punishment (Mill 1977b, p. 282). Throughout the essay, Mill seems to be attempting to narrow the conception of harm, so as to expand the realm of self-regarding liberty. By tying a causal and noncontingent link between the birth of a child and harm to the labor market, Mill shows his progressive, or future-regarding, concerns about the conditions of human flourishing. The birth of a child has no effect on its contemporary labor market; its effect will only—and possibly—be on the future labor market that the child will be entering. And yet Mill is willing to hold the parents morally and possibly criminally responsible for violations against this "distinct and assignable" obligations to future peoples (Mill 1977b, p. 281). This longitudinal conception of harm demonstrates not that it is broad and overly liberty-limiting, but rather that it is forward-looking, and derived from the interests of man as a progressive being.

CHAPTER FIVE

Progress and democratic theory

The various principles of Mill's liberal-utilitarian project are intelligible on their own. But in order to combine them into a coherent doctrine of reform, it is necessary to understand that Mill holds a longitudinal perspective on his moral and political prescriptions. His policies would enable individuals to develop their faculties and express their unique predispositions, which would over time, outweigh all of the utilitarian costs of implementing his policies. And as people approached his character ideal they would experience more, and higher, pleasure. This lifelong reasoning might seem tautological—like saying liberals will be happiest when they construct a liberal society—but underpinning his doctrine is the faith that humanity is gradually, unevenly, but ultimately evolving toward a European civilization where all would flourish. This *telos* is crucial, because as will be discussed in the next chapter, his entire project is only coherent with either a very particular and robust conception of human nature, or the presumption that all of humanity is evolving toward one ideal, Mill's Religion of Humanity.

Positivist history

From the point of view of history, Mill lived during some of the most momentous years in modern European History. Between Darwin, Marx, Napoleon III, political and philosophical events that would influence the development of Western Civilization were unfolding. Across Europe, the decline in the political and cultural power of the aristocracy, slowly created the opportunity for the reorientation of English society away from its backward-looking deference to antiquated social norms and culture, and toward more utility-producing ways of life. Amidst this background of uncertainty and potential, Mill was aware that he was living through an age of revolution (Mill 1986, p. 230).

In a series of articles entitled, *The Spirit of the Age*, published in the *Examiner* in 1832, Mill reflects on the progression of history. For Mill, one of the greatest achievements of the time was the widespread diffusion of "superficial" knowledge. The ability of more and more people to reflect upon their own beliefs, and to form reasoned opinions, was eroding some of the fundamental ideas and practices of Victorian England. The reason for the onset of this newfound critical reflection was the flowering of widespread discussion among the "reading and thinking" part of society (Ibid.). It wasn't that people were reasoning better, rather, it was that they were reasoning *more*. With discussion of all matters, both trivial and significant, came the eventual questioning. Society's deepest held ideas and beliefs were being reconsidered by a growing portion of society. Ultimately, the ideas and opinions that united and divided people's identities were collapsing.

> It is felt that men are henceforth to be held together by new ties, and separated by new barriers; for the ancient bonds will no longer unite, nor the ancient boundaries confine. Those men who carry their eyes in the back of their heads and can see no other portion of the destined track of humanity than that which it has already traveled, imagine that because the old ties are severed mankind henceforth are not to be connected by any ties at all. (Mill 1986, p. 229)

The question was what those new ties and barriers would be. Mill's entire doctrine of reform is his answer to this ontological question. Much could be learned about the future, and much could be done to influence it, because the seeds of all future periods exist in the present time.

Mill's conception of history and his theory of progress are the keys to understanding his liberal-utilitarian project. The very notion of progress is a hugely influential product of the Enlightenment, and filters into Mill's thought by way of French Positivism. Auguste Comte, and before him Saint-Simon, recognized that all natural phenomena were governed by uniform laws, and so considered the scientific method (or rather their scientific method) to be the only source of knowledge. What people once thought were uncontrollably random events, or the whims of divine intervention, were now understood as ordered events caused by their natural antecedents. It would therefore be possible to construct a *positive* science whose object of study was society. Emboldened by this faith in the explanatory and predictive potentialities of science, Comte sets out to understand the evolution of society, and chart its future development (Corser 1970, p. 3). Studying history, it would be possible to make inductive generalizations about the conditions that precede social phenomena, from which we could deduce principles to guide social policy. Comte was particularly interested in the conditions of social stability, and those of social change, which lead to his twin approach of social statics, and social dynamics.[1] Stability, which characterizes the "organic" states of history, are maintained by a consensus of opinion and mode of thinking. It wasn't simply a unanimity of values and belief, it was also the uniformity of the origins and the enforcing sanctions of such values and beliefs. As scientific knowledge challenges the consensus of opinion, the organic state eventually gives way to the next "critical" state of history, which lacks social and intellectual cohesion (Corser 1970, p. 8). This tumultuous disharmony reigns until a new system of values and beliefs ascends to establish a new consensus, and society enters the next organic state. What drives society from one period to the next is the growth and status of knowledge. As more natural and social phenomena are understood scientifically, old ideas are discarded as new ones slowly take root.

Mill was deeply influenced by Comte, even though he ultimately rejects and even ridicules the ultimate expression of Comte's positivism (Mill 1969d, pp. 263–368). One of the key ideas Mill takes on board is that a science of society was possible, and necessary in order to influence policy and guide reform. The science of society, or sociology, was an expression of the more general laws of psychology, and like ethology, it was far more complex, dealing with the interactions of many different factors. To begin with, it was necessary to identify the object of study, which would cut across culture and time. Presuming mankind to be both rational and social, Mill proposes focusing on indicators, such as:

> the degree of knowledge, and of intellectual and moral culture, existing in the community, and in every class of it; the state of industry, of wealth and its distribution; the habitual occupations of the community; their division into classes, and the relations of those classes to one another; the common beliefs which they entertain on all the subjects most important to mankind, and the degree of assurance with which those beliefs are held; their tastes, and the character and degree of their æsthetic development; their form of government, and the more important of their laws and customs. (Mill 1974, p. 911)

There exists a natural correlation between these aspects of any given state, such that they all tend to evolve in tandem with each other. In the earliest stages of civilization, these social phenomena were governed by independent natural forces. But over time, humans developed the ability to influence their natural and social circumstances, which in turn influenced the development of individual faculties and eventually individual character. Mill rejects the idea of metaphysical free will, but his belief in the causal determination of nature, leaves room for the individual to influence this reciprocal interaction (Mill 1974, p. 837). Humanity was thus not doomed to repeat the same states of history as natural circumstance determined, instead Humans could build upon and improve their circumstances and evolve into altogether new states of history. Mill possessed a faith in humanity that "the general tendency is, and will continue to be, saving occasional and temporary exceptions, one of improvement; a tendency toward a better and happier state" (Mill 1974, p. 914). This faith is the very foundation of his liberal utilitarianism, even though he concedes it is merely a theory. But like other complex theories, it was simply a matter of the developing the appropriate scientific method in order to verify. The method of sociology is called *Inverse Deduction*, or the *Historical Method* (Mill 1974, p. 917). There are enough commonalities between humans, and their natural circumstances to establish laws that govern the transition from one state of history to the next. The method requires first a detailed study of history in order to induce empirical laws of society, which are simply generalized observations about what social phenomena precede others. The purpose of sociology is to explain these phenomena using the (to be established) laws of ethology and ultimately, the most general laws of psychology. In this way, sociology was another *axiomata media*, connecting the more general laws of human behavior with the empirical observation and historical analysis of society. Like Comte, Mill is interested primarily in conditions of social stability, and the process by which a society moves from one state to the next, and so he adopts the focus on organic and critical states of history, but calls them natural and transitional states (Mill 1986, p. 252).

The primary characteristic of a transitional state is the inappropriateness of those wielding political, or "worldly" power, as Mill calls it. This disjuncture can be due to the decline and corruption of existing institutions, or the increase in the average intellectual development of the people. In either case, the wielding of worldly power is no longer done by the "fittest persons whom the existing state of society affords" (Ibid.). At the same time, disagreement increases between the intellectual leaders of society. The lack of uniformity in the exercise of this "moral power" is another characteristic of a transitional state of history. Greater access to education, and an enlarged realm of social and political space for free discussion (provided by the Principle of Liberty) has eroded old truths, but new ones have not yet emerged. There are subsequently no "established doctrines" organizing the thoughts and behavior of the people, as rival doctrines compete for allegiances of the governed (Mill 1986, p. 252). For most people in society, meeting their material needs consumed the vast majority of their time, and so lay people don't have the mental resources to evaluate the claims made by competing elites to judge their worthiness. Mill claims most of Europe is in such a transitional period, and so he is especially keen to comprehend the conditions of natural periods.

In the natural states, power is exercised without much resistance, because intellectual and political leaders are generally the ones most fit to lead. Whether qualified people ascend by force, or incumbent leaders become qualified, their leadership is accepted and unchallenged. Most importantly, all challenges to the exercise of this established power that arise are dealt with entirely within the established political and social structures. The progressive nature of human civilization means that every natural period enjoys social and political institutions that are uniquely appropriate for its time. Citizens do not chafe under the yoke of their government, nor do they feel alienated from the prevailing social norms and customs. This says nothing of the happiness, or welfare of the people, only that their system of government and social power are the most appropriate, given the level of intellectual development. Those exercising worldly power have no need to impede the progress of civilization because such progress poses no threat to their rule (Mill 1986, p. 252). In addition to there being unrivaled worldly power during natural states, there is also a dominant moral power. The sources of moral power are wisdom (or perceived wisdom), religion, and worldly power itself. Intellectual elites, who have made it their business to "investigate and study the physical, moral and social truths, as their peculiar calling", enjoy the uncritical deference by society, in part because of the consensus that exists between them (Mill 1986, p. 244). Mill's utilization of elites is found in several of Mill's other key writings, such as competent judges of *Utilitarianism*, and the more individualistic people of *On Liberty*. Natural periods of history entail general agreement among these three sources of moral power over the content of moral or scientific knowledge, or an unrivaled predominance of only one of these sources.

Natural and transitional periods in history are somewhat matters of dispute. But some are easily identified, and much could be learned from them about the sources of their conditions. During one of the great natural periods of European Civilization, Ancient Greece, the dominant power structure was able to sustain itself for so long because of the practice of selecting only virtuous and wise men as political leaders, thus combining worldly and moral power in the same people. This arrangement facilitated political stability, which enabled popular ideas to accumulate, take root in the minds of citizens, and grow up over the ages. Another natural state of note was Medieval Europe under the Catholic Church. For years, the Catholic Church was the only repository of knowledge and wisdom in society, and thus enjoyed a complete monopoly over moral power, and rightfully so. The Clergy were often the only literate people in a community, and the only source of knowledge. The combination of religion and wisdom in a single institution proved very stable, because even though the Clergy only professed authority in spiritual matters, political leaders sought their approval to help consolidate worldly power over their Christian citizens. Although Mill is highly critical of the morality of the Catholic Church (especially its overemphasis on asceticism and self-denial) and its eventual corruption, the Church played an essential role in the development of European Civilization (Mill 1986, p. 306). Eventually, as the Protestant Reformation weakened the Church's monopoly of authority over the political rulers and their citizens, Europe moved violently into the next transitional period.

> The more advanced communities of Europe succeeded, after a terrific struggle, in effecting their total or partial emancipation: in some, the Reformation achieved a victory—in others, a toleration; while, by a fate unhappily too common, the flame which had been kindled where the pile awaited the spark, spread into countries where the materials were not yet sufficiently prepared; and instead of burning down the hateful edifice, it consumed all that existed capable of nourishing itself, and was extinguished. The germs of civilization to come were scorched up and destroyed; the hierarchy reigned stronger than ever, amidst the intellectual solitude which it had made: and the countries which were thus denuded of the means of further advancement, fell back into barbarism irretrievable except by foreign conquest. Such is the inevitable end, when, unhappily, changes to which the spirit of the age is favourable, can be successfully resisted. Civilization becomes the terror of the ruling powers, and that they may retain their seat, it must be their deliberate endeavour to barbarize mankind. (Mill 1986, p. 307)

Mill is, of course, describing the rise of the French Empire under Napoleon. Another lesson from Revolutionary France: the progress of civilization can sometimes be stalled, perhaps indefinitely. The transition from one period to the next is not discrete: as the Church's power waned all over Europe, another stabilizing force was starting to emerge, the Aristocracy.

None of the Churches that emerged in the wake of the Protestant reformation commanded the moral power of the Catholic Church. In the absence of this overwhelming religious force, the English Aristocracy derived its moral power primarily from its worldly power. The Aristocracy lacked the supernatural grounding of their power that characterized the Catholic priesthood, but the

Aristocracy's power penetrated more deeply and pervasively into the person's daily life, regulating everything from morality to dress. Though the Aristocracy was not the repository of wisdom in England, any novel idea or innovation—of which there were few, according to Mill—required at least their tacit approval in order to be considered by the masses. The Aristocracy did contain, however, "a larger share of civilization and mental culture, than all other classes taken together," and so satisfied the conditions for exercising moral power during this natural state (Mill 1986, p. 314).

> Under their influence grew up the received doctrines of the British Constitution; the opinions, respecting the proper limits of the powers of government, and the proper mode of constituting and administering it, which were long characteristic of Englishmen. Along with these arose a vast variety of current opinions respecting morality, education, and the structure of society. And feelings in unison with those opinions, spread far, and took deep root in the English mind. (Ibid.)

Aristocratic dominance was the most appropriate order for the English people for many years, but by the early nineteenth century, the intellectual development of the citizenry had made them sensitive to the corruption of Aristocratic government, and challenges began to emerge to the consensus of their rule. As nineteenth-century France demonstrated with its dizzying series of regimes, universal suffrage before a people were ready for it would provide none of the benefits of democracy, and magnify all of its liabilities (Mill 1977a, p. 52). In order for English society to progress to the next natural state of history, individuals would need to further develop their intellectual capacities, and all relationships would need to be reorganized along more utility-producing lines. *The Subjection of Women* addresses the relationships within the family, *On Liberty* addresses the relationships between individuals, and now we turn to the relationship between citizens and their democratically elected government.

The theory of progress and democracy

Another positivistic aspect of Mill's conception of progress is the presumption that civilization is developing along a particular trajectory. History is not an account of the spontaneous mutations of society, rather, history provides evidence that knowledge and wisdom accumulate and propel society to higher states of organization and being. Like all Enlightenment thinkers, underpinning Mill's social thought is a particular conception of progress. Mill, like many people today, takes for granted that all civilizations are gradually converging on Western values and institutions. Once they do, general happiness could only be maximized by adopting Mill's principles. This hubris was understandable in the nineteenth century, as European colonialists confused modernization with Westernization. But today, the divergent ways in which developing countries have modernized potentially undermines the empirical sustainability of Mill's doctrine, as I will discuss in the next chapter. Nonetheless, this ultimate telos makes it possible and necessary for Mill to distinguish between more and less advanced societies of the world. In particular, using the indicators of a historical state, Mill differentiates between "barbarism" and "civilization."

> In Savage communities each person shifts for himself; except in war (and even then very imperfectly) we seldom see any joint operations carried on by the union of many; nor do savages, in general, find much pleasure in each other's society. Wherever, therefore, we find human beings acting together for common purpose in large bodies, enjoying the pleasures of social intercourse, we term them civilized. In savage life there is little or no law, or administration of justice; no systematic employment of the collective strength of society, to protect individuals against injury from on another; every one trusts to his own strength or cunning, and where that fails, he is generally without recourse. (Mill 1977d, p. 120)

As levels of social coordination increase, so too do wealth and mental development. Power in general, which resides in the hands of a few during barbarous states, becomes shared between growing numbers of people as society develops. Social cooperation and mental development are thus very closely related. This ability to coordinate is exactly what barbarous people lack, and makes them more like animals than humans. Social cooperation requires forgoing some immediate benefits for the enjoyment of a later ones, or benefits that one would share with others. This foresight and discipline is beyond savages as much as it is beyond the cleverest of the animals (Mill 1977d, p. 122). The progress of society is thus a civilizing as well as a humanizing process. Despite being a progressive reformer, Mill maintained a thoroughly Eurocentric conception of civilization throughout his writings: as societies in their nonage progressed, Mill thought they would come to look a lot like European societies. In fact, it should not be a surprise that he considered England to be the most civilized of all nations. He cites the prevalence of trade unions and the widespread availability of newspapers as evidence of England's preeminence (Mill 1977d, p. 125). But despite these achievements, England was in a state of transition and its progress to the next stage was uncertain.

In 1832, the United Kingdom passed the Reform Act, which, among other things, almost doubled the number of eligible voters. Democracy was spreading, and Mill recognized that most English people did not yet have the energy and independence of mind to take full responsibility for their political destinies. One of the hallmarks of civilization, as described above, is the growing interdependence of individuals to meet many of their vital needs. This division of labor has resulted in greater overall efficiency, which has yielded a vast surplus of human energy and time. The surplus energy has been directed toward a number of different ends, such as the pursuit of virtue, philanthropy, self-aggrandizement, or personal wealth (Mill 1977d, p. 129). The important point is that that these largely discretionary pursuits were purely matters of choice. The growing middle class, having enough comfort to feel secure, and enough education and development to harbor ambition, spent most of their time pursuing material wealth. The upper classes, on the other hand, having all of their needs met, and enjoying great wealth along with their accompanying feelings of self-importance, had come to possess less energy with which to direct toward these discretionary pursuits. Ultimately, the majority of people squandered their energy on selfish pursuits, or had none at all. Energy was not being invested in improving one's faculties and sensitivities, or in helping others develop theirs. Most troubling of all for Mill was that without energy, individuals were easily influenced by the homogenizing and stifling influence of the dominant social norms. This was the dilemma for Mill: the English people have outgrown the aristocratic form of government, but were not yet fully ready to embrace democracy. The key to progressing to the next natural state of history was to expand and promote democracy, while resisting the accompanying rise in mass society, as de Tocqueville warns in his essay on the United States. Democracy was now the necessary system of government, but the English still needed to increase the level of intellectual development, especially among the lower classes, in order to fully benefit from this type of political autonomy, instead of being overwhelmed by it.

Mill addresses the threat of individuality being crushed primarily in *On Liberty*, but many of his writings touch on this central feature to his moral and political thought. In a democracy, worldly power is exercised by the numerical majority, and so there are risks associated with deviating from prevailing social norms. Nonetheless, individuality is the source of the highest quality of pleasure, and is a permanent source of progressive energy.

> The despotism of custom is everywhere the standing hindrance to human advancement, being in unceasing antagonism to that disposition to aim at something better than customary, which is called, according to circumstances, the spirit of liberty, or that of progress or improvement. (Mill 1977b, p. 272)

Custom and tradition play important roles socializing individuals, especially with regard to morality. But during transitional states of history, dogmatically deferring to custom in all areas of life is a hindrance to the development of new social practices and ideas. Mill cites China as an example of a great civilization that has achieved much over the centuries, but has ceased to progress because of the high levels of conformity fostered by the educational and political systems. China, according to Mill, can at this point only develop as a civilization at the hands of foreigners (Mill 1977b, p. 273). Mill feared that England was liable to stop progressing because large portions of society were still under the sway of Aristocratic power. Mill laments the fact that the "moralists" and "general sympathizers of mankind" think that a passive character is better for society than an active one, because "Passive characters, if we do not happen to need their activity, seem an obstruction the less in our own paths" (Mill 1977c, p. 407). Mill concedes that active characters are capable of more evil, but they are also capable of more good: it is simply to possess *more* human nature (Mill 1977b, p. 263). Energy needs to be disciplined and channeled into utility-promoting ends. "Pagan self-assertion" and "Christian self-denial" are both elements of human flourishing (Mill 1977b, p. 266). Energetic and active characters are essential to resisting the homogenizing forces of custom and tradition, and so are the central aspects of Mill's character ideal throughout his writings.

No single form of government is universally appropriate for all people. Government needs to be appropriate for the level of intellectual and organizational development of the people. The people, then, are the largest factor in determining the quality of the government. This fact holds true for any government, whether it is democratic or not. Consider the very first duty of any government, providing justice for its people. Justice for primitive societies might not consist in much more than physical and material security. If the instruments for providing this essential service are drawn from the population, the personal qualities of these functionaries will matter more than the practical obligations of justice.

> Of what efficacy are rules of procedure in securing the ends of justice, if the moral condition of the people is such that the witnesses generally lie, and the judges and their subordinates take bribes? Again, how can institutions provide a good municipal administration, if there exists such indifference to the subject, that those who would administer honestly and capably cannot be induced to serve, and the duties are left to those who undertake them because they have some private interest to be promoted? (Mill 1977c, p. 389)

The rule of law is only as good as the people responsible for enforcing it. But even though the merits of any government are relative, humans universally share the same permanent interests as progressive beings (Mill 1977b, p. 224). Therefore, regardless of the state of history, all governments universally must perform two general functions. First, the government must protect the interests of its people, utilizing all the latent abilities of the people themselves. Second, and more importantly, the government must constantly work to promote the abilities of their people, specifically their "virtue and intelligence" (Mill 1977c, p. 390). The more autocratic a government is, the more distinct these two goals are, but as citizens take on more political autonomy, the more intertwined these two functions become. In a fully democratic, representative government, the institutions are merely the machinery, whereas the citizens are the power for that machinery, and more crucial for the overall welfare of the country. Whatever the level of development a country has achieved, a government must always strive to promote these two ends as its primary purpose.

Because so much turns on the quality of the character of the governed, Mill must make clear when a people are prepared for the responsibilities of representative democracy. First, a people must be willing to accept their government, or rather, they must not be so unwilling to receive their government that they actively attempt to subvert it. Second, the people must be willing to do what is necessary to maintain their government, namely obey the law, participate in political debate and cast deliberative votes. Third, the people must be willing to do what is necessary for the government to perform its two general functions of protecting their interests and developing their abilities (Mill 1977c, p. 376). Governments are neither purely matters of choice, nor are they spontaneous developments. Governments are in part an expression of a people's character, and as such, are partly the object of human will, and partly product of historical circumstance. It is difficult to know for sure when a society has met these criteria, but Mill was certain that the England of his day had reached a level of development that necessitated representative democracy. Like the Principle of Liberty, democracy was only appropriate when the people had reached a sufficient level of intellectual development that they could benefit from the social conditions it establishes. The English, though lacking in intellectual development among some of its classes, were nonetheless sufficiently developed to benefit from the responsibilities of representative democracy.

> It is by political discussion that the manual labourer, whose employment is routine, and whose way of life brings him in contact with no variety of impressions, circumstances, or ideas, is taught that remote causes, and events which take place far off, have a most sensible effect even on his personal interests; and it is from political discussion, and collective political action, that one whose daily occupations concentrate his interests in a small circle round himself, learns to feel for and with his fellow-citizens, and becomes consciously a member of a great community. (Mill 1977c, p. 469)

Despite the risks of prematurely embracing democracy too broadly, remaining under Aristocratic dominance, both politically and socially, was clearly an outmoded system of organization for the English. In fact, representative democracy was not merely the most appropriate for the nineteenth-century England, it is the best possible government overall.

Representation and interests

It is commonly asserted that the best form of government would be the rule of a purely benevolent dictator. A sovereign with complete autocratic power could balance competing interests impartially, without making any of the suboptimal compromises that are necessary for democratic participation. Such a ruler, being perfectly benevolent, would never be corrupt, putting the interests of itself and its cronies above those of the general good. The problem with this hypothetical ideal, as Mill points out, is that it would fail to succeed in performing the two functions of government. First, the dictator would need to have omnipotent knowledge of all people's interests in order to properly promote them. Second, even if this knowledge were available, promoting the people's well-being for them would result in passive citizens with atrophied faculties of mind. Representative government is best specifically because it excels at performing the two functions of government simultaneously. The reason representative government excels is because of two sociological principles—first, that individual rights and interests are only fully secure when the individuals take responsibility for them; and second, that the level of overall happiness is proportional to the number and variety of people actively promoting it (Mill 1977c, p. 404). These sociological principles are themselves the extension and synthesis of two theories about human nature—that most people are partial to themselves and to their nearest friends and family, and that it is not possible to truly know what is in another's best interest, despite one's best effort.

> We need not suppose that when power resides in an exclusive class, that class will knowingly and deliberately sacrifice the other classes to themselves: it suffices to that, in the absence of natural defenders, the interest of the excluded is always in

danger of being overlooked; and, when looked at, is seen with very different eyes from those of the persons whom it directly concerns. (Mill 1977c, p. 405)

This claim has significant implications for Mill's theory of government, and for *every* representative government. The *epistemic privacy* of interests (to borrow the phrase), meaning the inability of any group to fully comprehend the interests of any other group, means that in order for the government to successfully protect and promote everyone's interests, everyone must be represented in the representative Assembly. Mill does not elaborate on the concept of representation, but his thoughts have foreshadowed some recent discussions about representation.

Much of the recent work on representation has been shaped by the work of Hannah Pitkin. In her book, *Theories of Representation*, she describes four different conceptualizations of representation (Pitkin 1967). *Formal* representation is simply the designation of one (or some group of people) to act on behalf of others. A key feature of this concept is the authorization that the representative has to act, along with the accountability to the represented. Authorization is the manner by which the representative achieves her position, such as by winning an election, and accountability refers to the mechanism by which a representative can be censured or removed by the represented. *Descriptive* representation is when a person or group shares the same qualities or characteristics as the represented, such as profession, race, or disability. This concept says nothing about what the representative does, merely that she share some of the descriptive commonalities as the people she represents. *Symbolic* representation is when a person, group, or object stands in for another group, such as when a head of state visits another country, or when a soldier salutes a flag. Finally, *substantive* representation is when the representative actively promotes the interests of the represented. In Pitkin's terminology, Mill is using a substantive conception of representation.

> Every elector who voted for him, would have done so either because, among all the candidates for Parliament who are favorably known to a certain number of electors, he is the one who best expresses the voter's own opinions, or because he is one of those whose abilities and character the voter most respects, and whom he most willingly trusts to think for him. (Mill 1977c, p. 455)

If we combine this passage with the above one, it seems Mill draws a very close connection between descriptive representation and substantive representation. Because of the epistemic privacy of interests, a representative could only fully understand her constituents' interests by sharing some of their defining qualities. For example, a representative could never fully understand the subtle and pervasive discrimination that minorities often experience, unless she herself was a minority. Mill does not use these two terms, but it is clear there is a strong, and possibly necessary link between these concepts. Recent scholars have, in fact, demonstrated a high correlation between these two types of representation (Davidson 2011, p. 211).

The role of trust raises another question for Mill's concept of representation. Even if a representative shares qualities with her constituents, there may still be substantial disagreements over policy. To what extent should a representative be bound by the opinions of the represented? This issue is cast as representatives acting as delegates versus acting as trustees. Delegates merely transmit their constituents' preferences to the legislative Assembly, and act to promote them. Trustees are empowered to act and make decisions on behalf of the constituents, irrespective of their opinions and preferences. Pitkin addresses this question by identifying a range of positions between the opposite poles of delegate and trustee. Ultimately, she concludes that because representation implies the promotion of the constituents' interest, there should not be a conflict between obeying the constituents and being completely independent of them. If there is a conflict between what the representative thinks is best, and what the constituents want, then no generalization can be made about settling the conflict. Such conflicts can only be settled on a case by case basis, depending on the empirical particulars of the disagreement (Pitkin 1967, p. 166). To this point, Mill considers if it is necessary for voters to demand pledges from candidates. For him, this question is not one of constitutional arrangement, but one of constitutional *morality*, or how representatives should behave (Mill 1977c, p. 504). Leaving the law open on this point allows voters to make their representatives either delegates or trustees. But Mill presumes that representatives will be generally much more intelligent than voters, and so representatives should be allowed as much independence as possible. Constitutional morality would seem to oblige voters to search for candidates of such caliber that they can be trusted with complete independence. Candidates, for their part, are obliged to make as many of their important political opinions known during the campaign. Pledges by representatives to do or forbear from some course of action would only be necessary if there existed some conflict of interest between the representative and some particular person or organization. Ideally, voters should be electing MPs that they trust to promote the welfare of the entire country impartially, but as will be discussed below, Mill is acutely aware that under a parliamentary system, voters do not have that luxury.

How well the government performs turns in large part on the quality of the representatives serving in the national Assembly. The major institutional problems that can afflict government are twofold: negative problems are institutions and offices with insufficient power to perform the two functions of government, and ignorant or generally deficient citizenry; on the other hand, positive problems are incompetent, under-achieving representatives, or corrupt representatives (Mill 1977c, p. 435). Mill is not using the word "corruption" here only to mean unlawful or fraudulent, instead he is using it in its classical sense, meaning contrary to the common good. All people have a range of different, and sometimes competing, interests. Some individual interests are compatible with the common good, while others conflict with the common good. For Mill, it is dangerous to talk of "real," as opposed to "mistaken" interests; instead all people choose which of their interests they act upon. The choice of which interests to pursue is a reflection of one's character.

> What is in a man's interest to do or refrain from, depends less on any outward circumstances, than upon what sort of man he is. If you wish to know what is practically a man's interest, you must know the cast of his habitual feelings and thoughts. Everybody has two kinds of interests, interests which he cares for, and interests which he does not care for. Everybody has selfish and unselfish interests, and a selfish man has cultivated the habit of the former, and not caring for the latter. Everyone has present and distant interests, and the improvident man is he who cares for the present interests, and does not care for the distant. It matters little that on any correct calculation the latter may be more considerable, if the habits of his mind lead him to fix his thoughts and wishes solely on the former. (Mill 1977c, p. 444)

This subjective valuation of interests does not mean that the choice of interests to act upon is completely beyond criticism. Mill makes clear that the dispositions to act on selfish and short-term interests are themselves evil. All individuals possess interests in security and justice, just as they have interests in appreciating the higher pleasures and expressing individuality. It is an empirical fact for Mill that all (developed) humans have these interests, and Mill's social reforms attempt to direct all of the formative influences of society to instill recognition of these essential interests. But the greatest evil of all, which Mill repeatedly warns against, is promotion of narrow class interests, over the general interest. As far back as Ancient Greece, and continuing through Victorian England, the concern of class legislation was primarily of the vastly more numerous working classes democratically passing laws that would weaken the property rights of the minority aristocracy. The evil of class legislation is further exacerbated by the fact that power corrupts. Once a person, or group, acquires power, their own personal interests take on a new importance. Mill is not content to let the constitutional morality of the representative alone prevent this type of abuse. As he puts it, "Governments must be made for human beings as they are, or as they are capable of speedily becoming" (Mill 1977c, p. 445). To deal with this threat, Mill employs two strategies to prevent this type of corruption of the governing process—near universal suffrage, and continuing development of the intellects of voters.

Suffrage

The sociological fact that individuals are best at promoting their own rights and interests, combined with Mill's utilitarian commitment to maximizing general happiness, would seem to require universal suffrage for all people. But this was too dangerous for Mill, because the vastly more numerous working classes were too partial to their short-term interests. A balance needs to be struck between the risk of class legislation, and the loss of democratic legitimacy and utilitarian maximization. Perhaps not surprisingly, Mill leans pretty far in the direction of universal suffrage:

it is a personal injustice to withhold from any one, unless for the prevention of further evils, the ordinary privilege of having his voice reckoned in the disposal of affairs in which he has the same interest as other people. If he is compelled to pay, if he may be compelled to fight, if he is required implicitly to obey, he should be legally entitled to be told what for; to have his consent asked, and his opinion counted at its worth, *though not at more than its worth* (emphasis added). (Mill 1977c, p. 469)

Mill here employs classic contractarian reasoning, despite his rejection of the social contract as a source of original political obligation (Mill 1977b, p. 276). What Mill is really appealing to here is the demand of justice that the state give each opinion proportional consideration, even if the Assembly rejects their preference. Despite this obligation, Mill acknowledges that there are grounds for disenfranchisement. Voting is not a right that all possess to do with as they feel. Voting is a trust, and as such, can be prudently restricted from certain groups of citizens.

In order for democracy to maximize the promotion of individual and general interests, each vote cast must represent the process of deliberatively assessing what one takes those interests to be. There are some groups of people, who for circumstantial reasons, are not capable of rational deliberation and so are disqualified from suffrage. If one's income does not meet the minimum threshold for taxation, then they should not be able to vote. Even though Mill recognized that such groups do pay various forms of sales tax, poor people do not have sufficient incentive to vote for fiscally prudent candidates. It costs such voters nothing to elect candidates who promise huge building projects and generous social services. Following this logic, Mill endorses some system of poll taxation, or flat fee in exchange for the opportunity to vote. As offensive as this may seem to our contemporary standards of political autonomy, Mill never considers the possibility that a poll tax might be prohibitive to lower income citizens, or could be used to systematically disenfranchise certain voters. For Mill the logic of such a financial contribution was clear, "that so every one might feel that the money which he assisted in voting was partly his own, and that he was interested in keeping down its amount" (Mill 1977c, p. 472). Similarly, if one was receiving poor relief from the state for their subsistence, they were also disqualified from voting: "He who cannot by his labour suffice for his own support, has no claim to the privilege of helping himself to the money of others" (Ibid.). The responsibility of voting is a form of power over others, so if one does not have the wherewithal to care for themselves, then they cannot expect to have this power over the affairs of others. Both of these disqualifications Mill considers to be temporary. They are meant to be remedial measures that motivate the indolent to improve themselves to the point of being able to participate in the political process. They are also intended to make sure that all voters have the same interest in fiscal responsibility. With the enfranchisement of large numbers of middle and working class workers after the Reform Act of 1832, it was especially important to prevent the terms and conditions of poor relief from becoming too generous. But ultimately, suffrage alone cannot eliminate the risk of class legislation; the continuing development of the characters and intellects of the entire population is the only way to ensure the impartial balancing of competing interests in a democracy. Ignorance and selfishness are the qualities that lead to class legislation—two aspects of a person's character that would be hard to factor into the qualifications for voting. However, one practical way to minimize the influence of these vices was to require literacy. Nobody would think to allow a child to vote-a child possesses neither the ability to understand complex political problems, nor the ability to articulate their particular interests. Similarly, an illiterate person cannot fully participate in discussions about politics in order to democratically negotiate policy. For Mill, there is no injustice in this requirement, because it is a "solemn obligation" that society should make education available to all (Mill 1977c, p. 470). Free expression and honest deliberation are the necessary conditions for the growth of knowledge, as discussed at length in Chapter II of *On Liberty*. It is for this reason that Mill opposes the secret ballot (Mill 1977c, p. 491). Mill thought the open ballot facilitated discussion among the public. It also prevented voters from voting selfishly, because they could be held accountable by their fellow citizens. But for Mill, it is: essential that the people who are entrusted with suffrage have a minimal understanding of the world, and everyone shares the same incentives and disincentives when it comes to policy. Mill's utilitarian commitment pulls him in the direction of universal suffrage, but his fear of widespread selfishness, expressed in class legislation, leads him to elitism. Infamously, Mill thought it possible to reconcile this tension in a system of plural voting.

In any cooperative human endeavor, expertise is identified and afforded more consideration than inexperience, and governments should do no different. The problem with government is that power attracts ambition, and can corrupt good intentions. One lesson that Mill takes from de Tocqueville's essay on nineteenth-century American democracy is that power-hungry candidates will pander to the masses in order to get into office. Politicians are also willing to exploit differences in society to their advantage, and most voters are often unable to see through this manipulation, often obliging such ambitions (Mill 1977c, p. 469). In any given electorate, the smaller number of more enlightened voters who can perceive the short-sightedness of supporting such candidates are routinely outvoted. The risk of this all-too-common outcome unfortunately correlates with expanded suffrage in democracies with relatively low levels of public education, such as Victorian England. Because Mill sees a close connection between democratic participation and the development of faculties, he proposes a system of voting that institutionalizes greater influence for intellectual elites.

When two persons who have a joint interest in any business, differ in opinion, does justice require that both opinions should be held of exactly equal value? If with equal virtue, one is superior to the other in knowledge and intelligence—or if with equal intelligence, one excels the other in virtue—the opinion, the judgment, of the higher moral or intellectual being, is worth more than that of the inferior: and if the institutions of the country virtually assert that they are of the same value, they assert a thing which is not. One of the two, as the wiser or better man, has a claim to superior weight. (Mill 1977c, p. 473)

One of the most infamous and controversial aspects of all of Mill's writings is this proposition that more intelligent voters should be given more votes than voters with less intelligence. Mill is trying to institutionalize an electoral counter-balance against the uninstructed majority voting into office candidates who would promote short-term interests, or worst of all, promote the interests of a particular social class. At the same time, he is careful to avoid a different sort of class legislation, that of the educated elites (Mill 1977c, p. 476). Mill does not specify how much more weight the vote of the more intelligent should have, but like many of his radical proposals, the specifics of implementation are open to discussion. He is clear, however, that the upper limit of the number of votes of the intelligent should not be so great as to completely outweigh the votes of the less intelligent. Such a proposal may seem a violation of Mill's commitment to justice, but for Mill, there is a categorically moral distinction between denying some people the vote, and giving others plural votes.

> Entire exclusion from a voice in the common concerns, is one thing: the concession to others of a more potential voice, on the ground of greater capacity for the management of the joint interests, is another. The two things are not merely different, they are incommensurable. Every one has a right to feel insulted by being made a nobody, and stamped as of no account at all. No one but a fool, and only a fool of a peculiar description, feels offended by the acknowledgement that there are others whose opinion, and even whose wish is entitled to a greater amount of consideration than his. (Mill 1977c, p. 474)

Justice requires that each voter has an equal voice to express their opinions through their representatives in the legislative Assembly, not that everyone has equal influence. As stated before, a necessary condition for using intelligence or literacy as a basis for distributing any benefit is that education be available to all people. With suffrage expanding faster than intellectual development, it was crucial to protect the enlightened minority. It is specifically the opinions of intelligent voters that are most often excluded from deliberation in the Assembly, which would never happen in any other cooperative endeavor.

Mill recognized that the system of plural voting as he conceived of it was unlikely to be adopted (Mill 1977c, p. 476). An obvious challenge for any intelligence-based system of distribution is how to measure intelligence. Ideally, a country would have a national curriculum and a "trustworthy system of general examination," which could be used to examine intelligence directly. In the absence of these being made available to all, Mill proposes using occupation as a test (Mill 1977c, p. 475). Again, Mill is sketchy on the details, but he claims that some professions require more intelligence than others. The larger and more complicated the interests involved in some work, the more intelligence the worker can be presumed to possess. Mill specifies a foreman as being generally more intelligent than laborers, skilled more intelligent than unskilled tradesmen, and bankers and merchants more than tradesmen (Ibid.). The passing of university examinations was another possible test of intelligence that warrants plural voting. The one measure that Mill is explicit about not using is wealth, because he recognized that "accident has so much more to do than merit with enabling men to rise in the world" (Mill 1977c, p. 474). Granting plural voting based on wealth would therefore be unjust, but it would also not serve its purpose because there is not a sufficient correlation between the wealth and intelligence. However, there was a de facto system of plural voting by virtue of the fact that some wealthy people owned several homes, and could therefore cast votes in several constituencies. Interestingly, Mill proposes to end such a practice *only* when a better system was put in place to assess the intellectual qualifications of voters (Mill 1977c, p. 476). What this suggests is that so strongly does Mill feel about the necessity of counter balancing the mass of uninstructed votes that he is willing to allow the temporary risk and injustice of conferring plural voting based on wealth. What is clear about this voting scheme is that it is consistent with the logic of Mill's liberal-utilitarianism, and its underlying conception of progress. Democratic deliberation, much like deliberative choice-making described in *On Liberty,* or the development of the capacities to appreciate the higher pleasures in *Utilitarianism,* are important, utility-maximizing procedures in themselves, but only if they lead to specific outcomes. The procedure of rational deliberation in one's life, just as in the representative Assembly, only has instrumental value if it leads to the correct life-choice or policy, for the correct reasons. As has been discussed in Chapters 3 and 4, Mill formally and informally appeals to the knowledge of elites to help individuals develop their own faculties, and maintain social progress by constantly challenging reigning orthodoxies in all areas of life. This deference to expertise and knowledge is in part why Mill has been accused of being an elitist.[2] But these readings miss the nuanced influence elites naturally exercise over individuals. Mill rejects the imposition of preferences on people, but he repeatedly endorses deference to intellectual authority. The scheme of plural voting should be seen as one of the few formal institutions of their subtle influence. It should be stressed that, like the other forms of influence elites exercise, plural voting constituted only a limited influence. It only allows elites to have a disproportional voice in the legislative deliberation, it fosters no ability to determine policy. Scholars dispute whether Mill retreats from his scheme of plural voting later in life, but it nonetheless remains consistent with his larger doctrine.[3] Regardless of Mill's ultimate commitment to plural voting, he proposes a new electoral system that also performs the function of promoting the quality of deliberation in the Assembly—Thomas Hare's system of personal representation.

Hare's system

The need for plural voting in England was in part to mitigate the effects of the electoral system in place. Mill points out that democracy in his time has meant two very different systems. On the one hand, pure democracy entails that all citizens are themselves also legislators. This system is one of equality because everyone has an equal voice in the deliberative process. On the other hand, single member district voting entails the exclusive rule of the majority over everyone else. Single member districts, used in such countries as the United States, the United Kingdom, Canada, and New Zealand, work by dividing the entire country into discrete electoral districts. Each district holds a vote and the candidate who receives a majority of votes wins. If no candidate wins an outright majority within the district, a mere plurality is sufficient in some countries (e.g. the United States of America, and the United Kingdom), in other countries (e.g. French Presidential elections) a second run-off election takes place between the top two candidates to produce a winner. In countries that have primarily two parties, such as in the United States, the winning candidates in each district usually gets a majority of the votes. But, in countries where there are three or more major parties, such as the United Kingdom, the winning candidate usually only receives a plurality of votes. Regardless of how small the numbers of votes are, as long as there is a plurality, then that candidate is the winner. The problem with this system is that it tends to produce an Assembly that over-represents majority party, and under-represents minority parties, or excludes them altogether. And because of this over-representation, often the members of the Assembly that determine legislation actually only reflect the views of a minority of voters, overall.

> Suppose then, that in a country governed by equal and universal suffrage, there is a contested election in every consistituency, and every election is carried by a small majority. The Parliament

thus brought together represents little more than a bare majority of the people. The Parliament proceeds to legislate, and adopts important measures by a bare majority of itself. What guarantee is there that these measures accord with the wishes of a majority of the people? Nearly half the electors, having been outvoted at the hustings have had no influence at all in the decision; and the whole of these may be, a majority of them probably are, hostile to the measures, having voted against those by whom they have been carried. It is possible, therefore, and not at all improbable, that the opinion which has prevailed was agreeable only to a minority of the nation, though a majority of that portion of it, whom the institutions of the country have erected into a ruling class. (Mill 1977c, p. 449)

In other words, a majority (the elected representatives) of the majority (voters) can end up being a *minority* of the country overall. This outcome is an extreme possibility. The much more common outcome is disproportionate representation given to the majority party, and the marginalization of minority parties.

In the three district country described in Table A, observe how the Z party candidates have won in each district, yielding an Assembly that is held by 100 percent of the Z party, even though only 57 percent of the entire country are Z party voters. Current research confirms that countries that use single member district schemes have higher percentage of disproportionality between the votes cast nationwide, and the resultant make-up of the Assembly (Lijphart 1999, p. 163). An advantage to single member district voting is that it tends to keep politics local and personal. By dividing the country up into constituencies, which then select their own representative, local communities can generate their own candidates who can then address local concerns. But again, Mill is primarily concerned that

Table A

	District 1	District 2	District 3	Total popular vote
Party X	15.00%	33.00%	5.00%	17.00%
Party Y	30.00%	33.00%	15.00%	26.00%
Party Z	55.00%	34.00%	80.00%	57.00%

the preferences of the uninstructed will be overrepresented, not that there will be a disconnect between voters and representatives.

Today, the major alternative to single member district voting is a system of proportional representation. In such systems, the country is not typically divided into constituencies. Instead, ballots list all of the registered parties contesting the election, and voters select a party. All of the votes for each party are counted, and then seats are allocated based on the proportion of the total vote each party receives. There are different versions of proportional representation, but broadly speaking, their emphasis is on parties, as opposed to candidates. Mill disparages politics that is too party-oriented, because "we do not choose that all the opinions, feelings, and interests of all the members of the community should be *merged* in the single consideration of which party shall predominate" (Mill 1988, p. 182). Mill thinks the character of the candidate is much more important than their party affiliation, and that should be the sole determinant of voting. Party affiliation is only a secondary consideration after the specific opinions and virtues of a candidate. The major advantage of proportional representation is that the party make-up of the Assembly usually correlates very highly with the percentage of votes that each party receives, and thus is a better mirror of the opinions of voters. Nonetheless, it often obscures the particular attributes of the candidates themselves, and reinforces party allegiances.

Mill endorses the system of personal representation first proposed by Thomas Hare. Hare was a contemporary of Mill's, and a civil servant in her British government. His system is a mix of proportional representation and single member district voting, and today is known as Single Transferable Voting (SVT). It is a complicated system, so I will just briefly explain the main features of it. In this scheme, the country is divided up into districts of equal population by dividing the total population of the country by the number of seats in the representative Assembly. Each district would generate their own local candidates, perhaps some belonging to national parties, others independent. The number of voters in each constituency is the quota of votes that each candidate must receive in order to be seated in the Assembly. Voters would each receive an extensive ballot naming all of the candidates running in all of the districts, and would rank their preferences for as long as they choose. The first advantage of this system is that a voter can cast her vote for any candidate standing in any district. she is not limited to the candidates standing in her district, even though she might be more familiar with them. Vote allocation takes place in several stages, each containing several rounds. In the first round of the first stage, votes are allocated to every voter's first choice candidate. Once a candidate receives their quota of votes, regardless of from which district the votes come, they are seated in the Assembly, and the specific voters who contributed to their election are likewise finished. All of the additional votes for candidates who have met their quota are returned to their ballots until the next round. Those candidates who have not met their quota in the first round retain their votes to see if they meet their quota in subsequent rounds. In the second round, all of the voters who have had their superfluous votes returned to them in the first round cast their vote for their second choice candidate. Again, once a candidate receives their quota, they are seated in the Assembly, and the third round proceeds in like manner. This process repeats until all superfluous votes are allocated. The key to understanding Hare's system of personal representation is the ability to switch between the candidate's perspective and the voters' perspective. The next stage of the process eliminates the candidate with lowest number of votes. The votes for the eliminated candidate are returned to their original ballots, and the voters redistribute these votes to their second choice candidates. This process of eliminating candidates and redistributing the votes cast for them continues until every seat in the Assembly is filled with representatives who have met their quota. If every voter's preference list of candidates is sufficiently long, then every single voter will have directly contributed to electing a member of the Assembly, and can claim to have representation.

Single member district systems of voting have some distinct failures that impede their ability to produce Assemblies of the highest caliber. To begin with each voter is limited only the slate of electors offered by the local party officials. This "Hobson's choice," as Mill calls it, is often no choice at all (Mill 1977c, p. 456). Conversely, the candidates having only their local constituents to persuade, often influence voters through other levers of local power they may possess. Finally, and most importantly, all those voters who cast their vote for the losing candidate essentially remain unrepresented in the Assembly. Hare's system more than overcomes these deficiencies. The key aspect of Hare's system is that voters can cast their vote for any candidate. Not only does that multiply the number of potential representatives for each voter, it also means that each candidate would have to endeavor to broaden their appeal beyond their local district. Moreover, because voters would prefer to cast their vote for local candidates, districts would be compelled to compete between themselves to recruit the best candidates to stand in their district. The primary benefit would be that minorities would be able to secure some representation in the Assembly. Whereas in single member district voting, anyone who does not vote for one of the major parties essentially throws her vote away, under Hare's system, these votes can be pooled together from different districts. Provided the number of supporters for the minority party was at least as large as the quota necessary to elect a candidate, they could be guaranteed at least one representative. Mill clearly has in mind intellectual elites. They are scattered around the country, and are routinely outvoted in their districts, but Hare's system enables them to pool their votes to elect at least a few members. Even though the country is divided up in to geographic districts, a representative's real constituency would be all of the voters who contributed to their quota, wherever they may live: "The member would represent persons, not the brick and mortar of the town" (Mill 1977c, p. 455). The fact that each voter directly contributes to the election of a representative would further strengthen the relationship between them and their constituent. A great deal of gratitude would, no doubt, be felt by the representative, who would have to worry about losing the support of every single one of his constituents.

Mill pushed hard for the adoption of Hare's system of personal representation, most notably in a speech to Parliament on 30 May 1867 (Mill 1988, p. 167). Yet, he recognized some difficulties with implementing the system; here I will mention just a few. To begin with, the system would require very complicated mechanisms to administer, such as a system for allocating votes to a candidate. A candidate may require [say] 100 votes to meet their quota and win a seat in the Assembly. If that candidate receives 150 votes, then some mechanism must be in place to determine *which* of those 150 votes will be used to fill that candidate's quota, and which will be returned to the voters. The mechanism could easily become politicized because such a determination would affect the other candidates in the subsequent rounds of vote allocation. Second, because votes can transfer to different districts, it is totally possible that a district ends up with no geographic representation. But for Mill, this is not really a problem because representation is about people, and not places. Some districts with special significance, like harbors, or other natural resources, might require geographic representation, and exceptions could be made for these areas. Finally, the whole system could easily be co-opted by an organized faction, or the larger political parties to the detriment of smaller political parties. For example, in each district, the party officials could prepare ballots with their candidates strategically ranked, and distribute them to voters. Personal representation requires voters to be extremely knowledgeable of the candidates nation-wide in order to work successfully. Many voters might simply opt to yield to the party line, rather than evaluate each candidate on their individual qualities and abilities. However, this is a risk that any scheme of voting is susceptible to, and so is not specifically a strike against Hare's system. In any system of politics, organized groups will be more effective than disorganized ones. In the end, perhaps recognizing its merits, and the fact that they stood to lose much upon the introduction of the system, the major parties during Mill's time resisted efforts to adopt Hare's system, and so was never put into practice.

The religion of humanity

Being primarily concerned with reforming every aspect of society, it is surprising that Mill in no place sets out a definitive vision of his ideal society. He provides specific moral and political prescriptions, but does not integrate them into an explicit Utopian vision. But this is not to say that he did not have such a vision. In private correspondences, and a posthumously published essay, Mill makes reference to a secular Religion of Humanity.[4] Mill's theory of progress implies the possibility that by adopting his policies, such a Religion would be possible. There are two important features of Mill's Religion of Humanity that warrant comment before concluding this chapter. First, it is primarily a set of thoughts and feelings about the relationship between the self and others, and second, it serves as the primary mechanism that maintains coherence in Mill's liberal-utilitarian project.

At the beginning of this chapter, I discussed Comte's influence on Mill, with regard to the science of sociology and his theory of progress. Comte's analysis of history also recognized the important role of the Catholic Church in maintaining a natural state of history. Its demise left a gap in the European mind that lead to period of great instability, most notably in France. Comte endeavored to fill that gap by recasting his positivist philosophy as a new religion. Instead of God, individuals would worship mankind (Wernick 2001, p. 188). Comte's own Religion of Humanity was unacceptable to Mill because the altruism at the heart of the theology was not merely an ideal sentiment but rather was the sole mode of conduct. Like Calvinism, every action was either duty or sin. Mill's utilitarian morality requires some level of altruism, but Comte's religion required complete submission to humanity. The "unity" and "systemization" that Comte's system describes completely obliterates individuality, as all conduct was aimed at the same end—the good of everyone *else* (Mill 1969d, p. 337). Whereas for Mill, general happiness is the test of conduct, Comte "committed the error which is often, but falsely, charged against the whole class of utilitarian moralists; he required that the test of conduct should also be the exclusive motive to it" (Mill 1969d, p. 335).

Mill also recognized the importance of religion in any natural state, but he rejects Comte's bizarre and illiberal positivist religion. Mill was trying to facilitate the next natural state of history with the Principle of Liberty, and with his moral and political prescriptions in general. Mill was trying to strike the right balance between uniting people under the power of law and public opinion, with a protected sphere of individual liberty. The first important feature of this Religion is that it entails individuals possessing a particular set of beliefs and desires about themselves and the world, which enables this balance. Different thinkers have sought to establish such a balance by employing various sentiments and institutions, but all have taken a parochial approach to this universal issue. Mill's historical analysis finds that all attempts to balance these competing interests have had three common features (Mill 1969f, pp. 133–4). The first feature is a system of education that instills discipline into its people. The first requirement of any society is for its people to be able to control their impulses and submit to law. Second, there must be a feeling of allegiance to some common objects, such as to God, a ruler, eternal laws, or even to principles. Whatever the object, it must be considered sacred, and infinitely more important than any individual. The third feature to balancing the law with liberty is a strong sense of cohesion. Here, Mill is talking about sympathy with one's citizens. As we discussed, the very notion of justice is only possible once a sufficient level of sympathy exists in a community, such that a wrong against one person is a wrong against the entire community. Only when individuals feel each others' pains and pleasures can the obligations of justice be upheld without collapsing back into crude expediency. In the great epochs of Western Civilization, Religion has played an important role in providing these three stabilizing sentiments in society, as it has been one of the central sources of moral power throughout history. However, Christianity could no longer serve this purpose. It no longer exercised the unrivaled moral power that it did during the Middle Ages because of its own historical follies, and the general intellectual advance of Europe. Now, the only way to accept Christianity and be moved to excellence is to restrain the critical faculties of the mind and willfully neglect the doctrine's many internal contradictions (Mill 1969e, p. 423). Moreover, Christianity is fundamentally a religion of selfishness. All religions that hold out eternal bliss as a reward for obedience, make it also the ultimate motivator of action, and thus "fasten down the thoughts to the person's own posthumous interests" (Mill 1969f, p. 422). For Mill, a new Religion needs to be established, in order to strike this balance between law and liberty, one that entails:

> A morality grounded on large and wise views of the good of the whole, neither sacrificing the individual to the aggregate nor the aggregate to the individual, but giving to duty on the one hand and to freedom and spontaneity on the other their proper province, would derive its power in the superior natures from sympathy and benevolence and the passion for ideal excellence. (Mill 1969e, p. 421)

Whatever institutions or principles of social conduct might bring this new Religion, it would entail a set of desires and beliefs about one's relationship with all other people. There was no doing away with religion. Instead, it needed to be refashioned so that it provided the three stabilizing forces of a free and stable society, while at the same time facilitating the continuing development of the distinctly human faculties.

The second important feature of the Religion of Humanity is that it would justify all of the utilitarian costs of maintaining his principles. Mill recognized that there are many different motives for acting morally or beneficently, and that ethics is primarily concerned with the consequences of action. At the same time, his understanding of psychology, and his commitment to associationism leads him to the lifelong commitment that certain motives could be instilled in every human being. Selfishness holds no privileged place in the mind over altruism. In the next chapter, we will consider the traditional critique that liberty and utility pull in opposite directions. It is conceivable that in order to maximize happiness, it might be necessary to apply the Principle of Liberty unequally, or to sacrifice the higher pleasures. The Religion of Humanity for Mill is a period in history when the selfish motives are habitually outweighed by the altruistic ones, and so such illiberal scenarios would, by the very definition of the Religion, not be possible. If sacrifices are necessary, there would be no shortage of individuals willing to sacrifice their own good for that of others, because the range of sympathy would span not just the nation, but the entire species.

> To call these sentiments by the name morality, exclusively of any other title, is claiming too little for them. They are a real religion; of which, as of other religions, outward good works (the utmost meaning usually suggested by the word morality) are only a part, and are indeed rather the fruits of the religion than the religion itself. The essence of religion is the strong and earnest direction of the emotions and desires toward an ideal object, recognized as of the highest excellence, and as rightfully paramount over all selfish objects of desire. This condition is fulfilled by the Religion of Humanity in as eminent a degree, and in as high a sense, as by the supernatural religions even in their best manifestations, and far more so than in any of their others. (Mill 1969e, p. 422)

Adopting Mill's moral and political principles would facilitate and maintain this Religion of Humanity, and it would also ultimately resolve all tensions between the standard of general happiness with all of its derivative principles, like the Principle of Liberty. For a community that fully adopts this Religion, or more likely, develops it over time, the amount and quality of pleasure would be so high as to outweigh all of the utility costs of bringing about this state of history. By arguing that Mill's doctrine of reform will bring about this kind of transformation, is the only way to defend against the traditional critique of Mill's project that posits a necessary tension between the commitment to liberty and the demands of utility maximization, as will be discussed in the next chapter.

Mill remarks that "Governments must be made for human beings as they are, or as they are capable of speedily becoming" (Mill 1977c, p. 445). Bentham and the Classical Utilitarians accepted humans as they were and endeavored to construct a system around their sensitivities to pleasure and pain. One of the consequences of Mill's mental breakdown was to move away from this static conception of human nature, and to make the improvement of mankind his ultimate goal. All of Mill's principles, policies and theories reflect his faith in the potential of the species, and the possibility of the Religion of Humanity.

CHAPTER SIX

Ongoing challenges

John Stuart Mill's comprehensive and systematic doctrine of reform leaves few gaps, and so offers several points for critical analysis. The foundation for Mill's doctrine is his experiential epistemology, and his inductive scientific method. By limiting the sources of direct knowledge to experience, Mill provides a powerful and self-evident foundation for its reliability. At the same time, this highly constrained epistemology proves insufficient to account for some complex mental phenomena, such as a coherent conception of the self, or the independent existence of matter. Perhaps most problematically, Mill's experientialism cannot account for the reliability of memory. For these difficult phenomena, Mill takes a "naturalistic turn," providing empirical evidence, rather than logical inference from experience, for the psychological reliability of these phenomena. Mill employs this same strategy for his "proof" of the ultimate value of happiness. The empirical evidence is derived from the principles of Mill's associationist psychology, which govern the interaction of ideas in the mind. Mill hoped these general laws of psychology would eventually come to explain all social phenomena, by way of the intermediate science of ethology. Ethology was to be the key to Mill's project of reform, because changing people's characters is the best way to really change people's behavior. A running theme throughout Mill's moral and political writings is the belief that developing a certain type of character—one that exercises the human faculties of choice in order to find a form of life that best conforms to one's unique predispositions—would provide for the greatest amount, and highest kind, of pleasure.

This character ideal represents one of the fundamental changes to Mill's inherited utilitarian doctrine. Bentham and James Mill took the individual's sensitivities to pleasure and pain as given, and attempted to construct a theory of government that arranges individuals in such a way so as to maximize general utility. Mill's project is far more ambitious: he aims to establish rules of conduct, and to construct institutions that would fundamentally change what people find pleasurable.

The best example of these revisions can be found in the arguments for the Principle of Liberty, which intends to demarcate a realm of social and political space within which every individual would be free to develop and express their individuality. Provided a person's action did not harm another person without their consent, they would be free to act. One of the challenges that has consumed much of the revisionary effort has been to define harm. Much turns on this effort, because a narrow conception of harm—perhaps one that only accepted bodily damage—would render the sphere of self-regarding liberty too large, thereby allowing all sorts of nonmaterial harms to be permissible. On the other hand, a conception of harm that is too broad would shrink the sphere of individual liberty to the point where no meaningful expression of individuality would be possible. Striking the correct balance is essential, because Mill recognized that within society there exists two conflicting forces: those that aim to impose the dominant social norms and values on everyone, primarily by moral coercion, which because of its pervasive and subtle effect, amounted to the "despotism of custom"; and those social elites who have developed Mill's character ideal and aim to help others reform their characters. As Mill states in the very first sentence of *On Liberty*, the essay is only concerned with social freedom. What this means is that The Principle of Liberty leaves open the possibility that individuals would experience high levels of influence at the hands of others, which could amount to "severe penalties." Provided these penalties are the "natural" and "spontaneous" consequences of the individual's actions, and are not coercive, then they are allowed by the Principle. The application of Mill's Principle is a matter of dispute within the literature. Unfortunately, his own examples of its applications do not provide unambiguous guidance.

Mill's principles can be understood in isolation, but in order to integrate them into his liberal-utilitarian doctrine, it is necessary to understand how they rely on a theory of progress. The level of intellectual development contained in a people is of crucial importance for determining the terms of social coordination. The Principle of Liberty only becomes appropriate when a people are "mature in their faculties" or capable of benefiting from free and open discussion. Similarly, representative democracy is only appropriate for a people once they are capable of rationally deliberating their collective and long-term interests. The ability to measure and compare the relative development of different civilizations using some common metric implies that there is one universal ideal toward which all civilizations are evolving. This ideal, Mill presumes, is the point at which it is necessary for the civilization to adopt his liberal-utilitarian principles in order to maximize their general happiness. Mill calls this inevitable destiny, the Religion of Humanity. Although not expressed in these terms, this theory of progress underpins Mill's doctrine, and enables him to argue that the ultimate benefits of his principles will outweigh their immediate costs.

The sympathetic presentation of Mill's liberal utilitarianism in the preceding chapters is another contribution to revisionary literature that seeks to integrate Mill's disparate writings into a coherent project of reform. This particular effort is not comprehensive, as it aims primarily to focus on certain key topics that are particularly difficult to understand, and integrate them into Mill's larger doctrine. In the interests of clarity, I have deferred most critical commentary of Mill's project to this last chapter. Controversy surrounds almost every major aspect of his thought, and so a full overview is beyond the scope of this book. Instead, I think two broad critiques warrant examination. First, the traditional critique of Mill's project, best articulated by Isaiah Berlin, questions whether a system of rights and the Principle of Liberty can be given a utilitarian foundation. This presentation of Mill's project relies heavily on Mill's theory of progress, which sees a universal convergence on European values and institutions, paving the way for the Religion of Humanity. I believe this last question—as to whether this convergence is empirically sustainable—to be an open one. John Gray argues that it is not. He makes the second critique, which is called the value pluralist critique. It is in part a restatement of Berlin's critique, but then extended to consider the future progress of different civilizations and a rejection of the universal convergence on one form of life.

The traditional critique

James Fitzjames Stephen, in his *Liberty Equality and Fraternity*, makes the very first systematic challenge to Mill's project (Stephen 1874). As a committed utilitarian himself, Stephen's book questions the need for specific principles, other than the Principle of Utility. What is the purpose of enshrining liberty in a distinct and predominant principle, if its value is purely instrumental and contingent on host of historical and political facts? Even though Mill repeatedly professes his commitment to utility as the ultimate standard, a close reading of *On Liberty* seems to reveal that there is more than just utility animating Mill's principles, especially the Principle of Liberty. The thesis that Mill accepts several ultimate values, in addition to utility, finds its most influential articulation in the work of Isaiah Berlin. Berlin celebrates Mill as the founder of modern liberalism, and as articulating the "classic statement of the case for individual liberty." However, Berlin argues that he fails in his life-long project of deducing liberal principles from the ultimate standard of utility (Berlin 1996, p. 132). He attributes to Mill a form of value pluralism, whereby competing and incommensurable values animate his moral and political prescriptions, which ultimately prove fatal to the coherency of his project. Berlin's essay has stimulated a huge body of revisionary literature on Mill that seeks to rescue the coherency of his project from Berlin's charge. Such projects are interpretative endeavors; and as such they draw upon the vast pool of published and unpublished writings of Mill to inform their interpretive. Alan Ryan, for example, argues that Mill's Principle of Liberty needs to be understood as governing only the moral department of the Art of Life, described in *A System of Logic* (Ryan 1996, p. 164). Another strategy has been to ascribe to Mill novel versions utilitarianism that can accommodate permanent commitments to liberty, such as Gray's attribution of indirect utilitarianism, or Wollheim's complex utilitarianism (Gray 1996; Wollheim 1996). I will not discuss such interpretations here, because the sympathetic presentation of Mill's thought in this book is itself a contribution to this body literature. Instead, it will be worthwhile to review Berlin's powerful challenge, because in the end, some his criticisms can be met, while others remain powerful and possible fatal.

Immediately following the articulation of the Principle of Liberty, Mill stresses that the self-regarding sphere contains, among others, two essential liberties—the freedom of thought and discussion, and the freedom to express individuality. His principle target in *On Liberty* is the dominant Victorian milieu and its defenders who sought to impose their behavioral norms and beliefs on open minded individuals deviating from the customary norms. The central claim necessitating these liberties, made forcefully in Chapters II and III of the essay, is that human knowledge is permanently incomplete and fallible. No matter how much empirical evidence one may have for a particular belief, it is always possible that new evidence will emerge that forces one to revise their belief, hence the permanent value of freedom of expression. Mill's supposedly empirical assessment of human nature, as being fundamentally creative and expressive, is harmed when forced to live a life not in harmony with its unique inclinations. Even if one was certain that they had discovered the best possible life for themselves, one could never be sure of what was the best life for anyone *else*, hence the permanent value of the freedom to express individuality. These permanent limitations in our knowledge necessitate liberty so each can pursue their own answers to their own unique questions. But, as Berlin points out,

> it may well be that without full freedom of discussion the truth cannot emerge. But this may be only a necessary, not sufficient, condition of its discovery; the truth may, for all of our efforts, remain at the bottom of the well, and in the meantime the worse cause may win, and do enormous damage to mankind. (Berlin 1996, p. 144)

If truth and falsity are equally liable to sink to the bottom of Berlin's well, then liberty moves society no closer to ascertaining the truth. Mill concedes that the only inherent power that truth has over falsity is that when suppressed, it is liable to be rediscovered in later periods (Mill 1977b, p. 239). If the liberty of thought and discussion is no guarantor that the truth will prevail, as Berlin suggests, then how can Mill maintain its necessity in the face of those who reject the fallibility of their own opinions, such as Victorians, religious bigots, and Bentham. Bentham shares Mill's empiricism, but not his skepticism about knowledge—certain essential truths could be known, such as one's sensibilities to pain and pleasure. From the utilitarian perspective, if there are significant utility costs to maintaining the liberty of expression then the uncertainty of the epistemological benefits might pale in comparison. It is not clear how racist or sexist expressions move us any closer truths about race and sex, and promote the growth of knowledge. For example, on 30 September 2005, the Danish newspaper *Jyllans-Posten* printed cartoons of the Prophet Muhammad, knowing full well the controversial nature of that act. Not surprisingly, Muslims around the world were outraged. Later, in 13 February 2008, the same cartoons were reprinted all over Europe in an attempt "to unambiguously back and support the freedom of speech."[1] According to Mill, because such offenses are not morally relevant to the Principle of Liberty (they do not set back the interests of justice), they must be endured. But if there are no clear utility gains in protecting certain offensive expressions, then such liberties would seem to lose their utilitarian justification. Whereas artistic expression can possess epistemological value, perhaps even when satirical, the reprinting of these cartoons seems to be nothing more than an attempt to inflict pain upon a minority group who reject that the purview of free speech should include blasphemy. This is not to say that there are *prima facie* reasons for censoring such offensive material, only that any utilitarian calculation would need to balance the utility gains of freedom of speech, against its utility costs. There are no *utilitarian* reasons to exclude the utility loss that sensitive believers experience when calculating the net utility of the freedom of expression, especially if there are no clear utilitarian gains. In order for the fallibility of human knowledge to necessarily require the freedom of expression, Mill's belief in the fallibility of knowledge must itself be infallible.

The fallibility of human knowledge entails several crippling disadvantages for any social theorist, including the lack of any universal truths, the fact that individuals and societies have their own unique pursuits that may not be mutually compatible, and the necessity of individuals reviving their pursuits in light of their experiments in living. And yet despite these epistemological limitations, Mill's entire project in *On Liberty* is based on one eminently knowable fact—human nature (Berlin 1996, p. 144). For Mill, humans possess unique inclinations that need to be expressed in order to be truly happy. These inclinations vary indefinitely, but the most amount of happiness is to be experienced by exercising the distinctly human faculties to discover or create a life that conforms to one's inclinations, and as such, yield higher pleasures.

Societies will vary in the relative development of their capacities, ranging from races in their "nonage" to England, but all societies can develop and evolve under the appropriate circumstances. From this universal nature, permanent interests can be deduced, enabling judgments of the relative progress of societies, as well as judgments about the appropriateness of their governments and systems of social organization. But Berlin rejects Mill's presumption of human nature because it is never expressly stated, is questionably supported by empirical evidence, and is a clear contradiction of Mill's commitment to the fallibility of knowledge.

> Yet within this framework of ideas and values, despite all the stress on the values of experiments in living and what they may reveal, Mill is ready to stake a very great deal on the truth of his convictions about what he thinks to be the deepest and most permanent interests of men. Although his reasons are drawn from experience and not a priori knowledge, the propositions themselves are very like those defended on metaphysical grounds by the traditional upholders of the doctrine of natural rights. (Berlin 1996, p. 146)

Mill conception of human nature is less an empirical conclusion, and more an ideal that he establishes around which to construct his thesis. Berlin's claim is that everything turns on this assumption: it not only holds his argument together in *On Liberty*, but also his entire liberal-utilitarian project.

Even if Mill's presumption about human nature is granted, his moral and political prescriptions in *On Liberty* do not necessarily follow. The picture of human flourishing that Mill depicts as an independent and active chooser with refined intellectual and moral sensitivities is "at best" only empirically connected to the self-regarding sphere of liberty (Berlin 1998, p. 200). There is no necessary link between this conception of human flourishing and the liberties of thought, expression, and individuality so forcefully argued in *On Liberty*. Given the ever-present human tendency toward mediocrity and conformity, individuals might require a dose of coercion from time to time to keep them on the path of self-development and introspective exploration, but Mill's explicit prohibition of paternalism rules out this plausible and possibly necessary strategy to facilitate his character ideal. In fact, there is ample evidence of Mill's character ideal emerging from highly disciplined societies, such as Calvinist Scotland or New England, according to Berlin (Berlin 1988, p. 200). Mill's purpose is to prevent people from elevating their mere dislikes to the status of moral disapprobation, and preventing harm to other people is the only grounds for interfering with a person's liberty. But if general happiness is the sole value underwriting Mill's project in *On Liberty*, then there may be instances when coercively interfering with liberty may actually promote this end. If we accept that Mill's conception of human nature is itself open to revision, like all other beliefs, then:

> It might be argued that there is no a priori reason for supposing that most men would not be happier – if that is the goal – in a wholly socialized world where private life and personal freedom are reduced to vanishing point, than in Mill's individualist order; and that whether this is so or not is a matter for experimental verification. (Berlin 1996, p. 147)

Mill's commitment to utilitarianism places him in a double bind in *On Liberty*: if Mill concedes that his conception of human nature is incomplete, then his particular vision of human flourishing holds no privileged place, and he would have to accept the possibility of the opposite vision being an equal or greater source of happiness for individuals. If Mill insists on his conception of human nature, then the necessary link between the infallibility of human knowledge and liberty is severed: the door is opened to other infallible truths about humanity that are exempt from empirical verification. Berlin's broader thesis is that however eloquent and attractive Mill's arguments for liberty are, he fails to erect them on top of a utilitarian foundation. What becomes clear from *On Liberty* is that Mill ultimately values diversity, liberty (to choose and to err), and individuality for *themselves*, independent of their contribution to general happiness.

If Berlin's criticisms hit their mark, then Mill's liberalism is not a species of utilitarianism, but instead an incoherent version of value pluralism. The centrality of individuality and the Principle of Liberty make clear that Mill is unwilling to make trade-offs between the two, and unwilling to compromise either for the sake of utility. Bentham, content that pushpins were as good as poetry, has no reservations making such trade-offs for the sake of general happiness. But this line of criticism is only valid if we exclude the very fact that underpins all of Mill's thought—his conception of human nature. Common experience may not support the conception of human nature that Berlin ascribes to Mill, but perhaps this nature is not so much the premise of Mill's argument, than it is the argument's end. A more empirical characterization of human nature is given in other writings, such as *An Examinations of Sir William Hamilton's Philosophy*, and *A System of Logic*, where Mill describes the laws of associationism. The picture of human nature that emerges from these writings is one of flexibility, malleability, and indefinite potential. Individuals, through parenting, education, and reinforced by religion, could be conditioned to experience the most happiness from this type of liberal lifestyle, just as easily from a different one. Mill's failed attempt to establish the science of ethology was specifically to discover how to move individuals in this direction. Evidence for this interpretation can be found in *On Liberty* where Mill describes how the mix of individual liberty and subtle influence by social elites would facilitate the development of this elevated human nature among the unreformed members of society. If we accept this conception of human nature, which is really a simplistic conception of human psychology, then it is possible to present Mill's overall liberal-utilitarian doctrine as coherent. However, the categorically different question as to whether his doctrine is empirically sustainable is, at best, an open question. There are three distinct questions here: whether the mind works the way Mill claims, if so, whether liberal society is the most expedient way to facilitate his ideal character, and most importantly, whether his ideal character, in all its indefinite manifestations, will in fact provide the greatest amount, and highest quality, of pleasure. If knowledge is fallible and incomplete, as Mill argues, then liberalism would be only one of several different practical arrangements that must be considered in the grand experiment in living.

The value-pluralist critique

One of the most thoroughgoing critiques of Mill's thought is made by John Gray. As a one time—though reluctant—defender of Mill, Gray offers an interpretation of Mill's liberalism as a species of indirect utilitarianism. Building on contributions to the revisionary literature, such as those by Ryan (1974), Rees (1996), and Berger (1984), Gray's interpretation of indirect utilitarianism enables Mill to maintain the Principle of Liberty (among others) as a constraint to utility maximization. Gray also ties Mill's conception of happiness very closely to individuality, such that a pleasure is higher for an individual if it is autonomously chosen and coheres with their individual nature. The last key feature of Gray's interpretation of Mill is that it is underpinned by a theory of progress about the conditions of self-development toward an ideal and universal character. This last aspect of his theory Mill shares with all Enlightenment thinkers, who also rely on such a conception, either explicitly or implicitly (Gray 1996, p. 15, 120). As I have stated at the outset, Gray's interpretation has been influential in my own depiction of Mill's thought in this book. However, in a second edition to his *Mill on Liberty: A Defence*, Gray reverses his position and argues that Mill's project is both incoherent and empirically unsustainable. Picking up on Berlin's attribution of value pluralism to Mill, he condemns not only Mill's project, but all recent variants of liberalism. Gray makes several criticism of Mill's project, some of them echoing the traditional criticisms made by Berlin, but others are novel and reflect his larger assertion of the failure of all Enlightenment ideologies. Rather than a broad overview, I will briefly discuss Gray's reversals of the main features of his own prior interpretation of Mill, before considering his larger critique of Mill, and the Enlightenment movement in general.

A society that adopts Mill's indirect utilitarianism has the paradoxical feature that utility will be maximized overall by not trying to directly maximize utility. That is to say, a society that adopts the Principle of Liberty as a rule will experience more utility than a society that appeals directly to the standard of utility to regulate social conduct, as the argument goes. But the Principle of Liberty supplies only the necessary condition and not the sufficient condition for when punishment is justified. Some nonconsensual harms to others are excluded from consideration by the Principle, such as harms that incurred in the market economy. As I have discussed in Chapter 3, such harms do not violate moral rights, because society has come to the conclusion over the years that it is more expedient for society not to punish such harms. When a person harms another person in such a way as to violate their rights, their own guilty conscious and the moral disapprobation of society are the minimum punishments required. Any further punishment imposed by the state is a matter of calculating the punishment's costs and benefits, i.e. appealing directly to the Principle of Utility. This is the point at which Gray argues the Mill's indirect utilitarianism loses its necessarily liberal character. Minor violations of the Principle of Liberty could be punished with disproportionately harsh punishments, should that prove expedient. Singapore's infamous punishment of caning for the crime of vandalism is an example of how the Principle of Liberty could allow a penal code at odds with most versions of liberalism. Moreover, there is nothing within indirect utilitarianism that would prevent widely unequal punishments across different segments of society for the same violation of the Principle. Gray points out that expediency might allow, or even *require*, that stricter punishments be imposed on minorities who might be predisposed to criminal behavior, or who might be simply discriminated against by the majority population. The Principle of Liberty does rule out some illiberal policies, such as interfering with someone's liberty when they are operating within their self-regarding sphere. But once a wrongful harm is committed against another person, however insignificantly, the severity of punishment is determined by the contingencies of expediency, not by some necessarily liberal principle.

The scenario Gray depicts is certainly a formal possibility in the application of the Principle of Liberty, but Gray neglects that the system of rights that forms the topology of the Principle of Liberty evolves from the individual interest of security to the communal interests of justice. What animates this evolution is the broadening range of sympathy members of the community have with each other, and the increasing recognition of complex and communal interests. Desert, being one of the interests of justice, entails an element of proportionality to it, whereby a disproportionately harsh punishment would be more harm than the offender deserves. Moreover, Mill declares impartiality the "first of judicial virtues," and the necessary condition for fulfilling all other obligations of justice (Mill 1969c, p. 257). Unequal punishments for the same crime would therefore be a violation of justice itself. The equal application of the Principle of Liberty, along with the equal moral and criminal sanctions would always be expedient because the shared sentiment of sympathy is one of the conditions for establishment of justice. Mill repeatedly states that what is just will also be expedient. Where the two differ is with regard to the "peculiar sentiment," derived from the basic instincts of sympathy and self-defense that attaches itself to justice (Mill 1969c, p. 259). To be clear, it is the sentiment that determines justice, and not the other way around.

Another feature of Gray's exegesis that he no longer thinks sustainable is his interpretation of happiness that entails exercising the human faculties of choice to choose a higher pleasure that best conforms to one's unique qualities. This criticism is directed not at the coherency of Mill's liberal utilitarianism, but at its empirical sustainability. If we grant Mill the presumption of his conception of human nature, then this peculiar conception of happiness necessarily follows. A lingering question about the coherency of Mill's qualitative utilitarianism is if the higher pleasures really are incommensurably superior to the lower ones, and that a rational person would always choose the higher over the lower. As I have discussed in Chapter 3, I think such incommensurability is a violation of Mill's hedonism, and that a rational person may choose the lower pleasure over the higher, if quantity so outweighed quality. As to the sustainability of the conception of happiness, Gray cites the practice of arranged marriages as a counter-example to Mill's conception of happiness. If exercising choice is a necessary element of happiness, then we would expect to find arranged marriages to be fundamentally less happy than marriages of choice, as an empirical tendency. Yet Gray claims that experience does not bear this out. In countries that have both practices, there is no significant difference between the outcomes of different types of marriages, and so choice cannot be a constituent element of (at least) marital happiness. However, I think the example of different marriage practices does not support Gray's claim about choice and happiness. Even though arranged marriages might preclude choosing with regard to marriage or not, and with whom, there is much subsequent choosing within the relationship. Couples in arranged marriages choose to build their relationships together, and anyone in a relationship will agree that this process involves a great number of very important choices sustained over a lifetime together. If there is no significant difference between the happiness of arranged marriages and marriages of choice, as Gray claims, then I would argue that the happiness between arranged spouses develops over time, as a product of the constant choosing to remain committed in the relationship. In fact, those couples who "fall" in love, or who are irresistible to each other form a relationship not as a product of rational deliberation, but of compulsion—the very opposite of choice. Nonetheless, I agree with Gray that experience demonstrates that there are many examples of happiness in which choice plays no part. If there is no necessary connection between choice and happiness, then Mill's conception of it would seem to be a non-empirically derived ideal, rather than a generic feature of human life. It must be remembered that Mill was surrounded by people who did not value choice; this was in part why he was writing *On Liberty*. He wanted individuals to resist the homogenizing influences of the dominant social norms in order to develop their faculties of choice, to experience more happiness. He was not deterred by the fact that his compatriots were content to conform to the dominant milieu, because underpinning Mill's doctrine of reform is a robust conception of progress. History showed Mill that all societies were converging on single universal form that entails liberal principles and privileged the faculty of choice. Gray's counter-example does not prove that happiness is independent of choice, and in fact there is recent evidence in psychology that suggests that a level of control and autonomy over one's life is an essential element of well-being (Tay and Diener 2011). And so, it may very well be the case that choosing comes to form a substantial element of happiness, as Mill implicitly argues. For Gray, this conception of progress, central to his interpretation of Mill, is subverted by the empirical truth of value pluralism.

There can be little question as to Mill's longitudinal perspective on human civilization. The progressive orientation of his project of reform is not merely an interesting feature of his thought, it is the ultimate justification for his liberal utilitarianism. Mill's Principle of Liberty becomes appropriate for a society only after it has achieved a certain level of development. Mill held that a high degree of social cooperation must be in place, such as commerce, and that individuals must be capable of spontaneous improvement by their own free discussion (Mill 1977b, p. 224). "Races in their nonage" were best ruled by a benevolent despot in order to prevent individuals from harming each other, and to facilitate their individual and collective development. Mill takes for granted that all societies were converging on a form of life that requires liberal democratic institutions in order to experience the greatest amount of utility. Mill could have posited the Principle of

Liberty and democracy as matters of natural right, or the products of a hypothetical social contract, but Mill rejects both of these foundations. Instead, he implies that the "permanent interests of man, as a progressive being" are propelling people toward this ideal. The central feature of Gray's argument is that this Enlightenment faith in the inevitability of all people gradually shedding their distinct and parochial forms of life, and adopting a universal and rational mode of existence that reconciles all rival goods, has failed. Gray, in large part, has come to this conclusion in the wake of the recent technological and economical development of East Asia, which has modernized to the point of rivaling the west, but without adopting Western values or institutions (Morgan 2007, p. 118). This provocative critique is, of course, hugely controversial, and I will not evaluate it here.[2] Instead, I want to spell out how the potential collapse of Mill's underlying conception of progress subverts his entire liberal-utilitarian project.

Several important aspects of Mill's doctrine of reform seem to lack sufficient empirical basis. What the theory of progress supplies are the conditions when such claims might be justified. For example, the claim that any rational person who has developed an appreciation for the higher pleasures will always prefer them is highly suspect. But it is clearly Mill's expectation that humans will eventually develop into the sort of people (like him) for whom this is true. In order to facilitate this transformation, it will be necessary to privilege the higher pleasures in the current society by, say, castigating people for indulging in the lower pleasures. But without the theory of progress to justify the superior desirability (in the descriptive and normative sense) of the higher pleasures, it becomes impossible for Mill to deduce and maintain such policies based on the ultimate commitment to utility. A much more fundamental problem is the claim that the Principle of Liberty, as the primary adjudicator of interests in society, is the most expedient principle to govern social conduct. As I have discussed, the coherency of Mill's project is based on his presumption about human nature. Without this, Mill's only recourse is to argue that people are progressing toward his ideal character type, at which point they will require the Principle of Liberty to experience the most amount, and highest kind, of pleasure. All of the utility costs of maintaining the Principle of Liberty today will be outweighed by the gains society will enjoy when it reaches this stage. But if this teleology is also empirically unsustainable, then Mill is left with no utilitarian justification for the utility-limiting Principle of Liberty. Mill's outright prohibition on paternalism is most conspicuously implicated in this failure. As I have discussed in Chapter 4, the freedom to err (e.g. experiments in living) and the necessity of incurring the consequences (e.g. severe penalties) are necessary means to developing the faculties of choice-making. If humans are not evolving toward the ideal character that privileges choice, then overall utility would clearly be maximized by interfering with some self-harming activities, such as dangerous narcotics. It's not that the lack of a theory of progress only allows Mill to make direct appeals to the Principle of Utility to guide conduct, for it may be the case that humanity is progressing differently, which then might justify different utility-limiting principles, other than the Principle of Liberty.[3]

In addition to subverting the utilitarian justification, the application of the Principle of Liberty also becomes problematic. Without the inevitable convergence on a single set of interests derived from the end of Mill's theory of progress, or his conception of human nature, it is impossible to adjudicate between different conceptions of harm. As I have presented Mill's theory, the interests relevant to the Principle of Liberty are those that have evolved from the universal interest of security to the complex and social interests of justice. But even these interests need a conception of human nature, or a conception of progress to operationalize. The absolute freedom of expression becomes equally legitimate as prohibitions on blasphemous speech if Mill's character ideal holds no privilege over the life of religious devotion. There would be no reason to exclude this type of harm from considerations of justice without one authoritative conception of human flourishing (derived from the theory of progress, or human nature) from which to derive practical interests. In fact, with several rival conceptions of human flourishing, it might be impossible to come to a consensus on the specific boundaries of the self-regarding sphere. If so, then Mill's Principle of Liberty fails to provide any practical guidance whatsoever. This indeterminacy points to, perhaps, the most damning failure of Mill's project without conceptions of human nature or progress— its inability to make interpersonal utility comparisons. If harm, beyond mere bodily integrity, is essentially contestable, then the Art of Life comes crashing down as it becomes impossible to make any utilitarian judgments whatsoever. There would be no way to compare principles of conduct, government policies, or even aspects of justice. If Gray's thesis about the empirical unsustainability of any conception of progress—again, a claim I am not assessing here—is correct, then Mill's project, even if coherent, lacks any empirical grounding for its moral and political prescriptions.

What, then, are we to make of Mill's project? Even if the coherency of his liberal utilitarianism can be defended with either the presumption of a robust conception of human nature, or a particular conception or progress, the fact that the entire project is not empirically sustainable surely delivers a coup de grace to Mill's lifelong endeavor. Or does it? Assuming Gray to be correct about the fallacy of progress, then the primary element that is lost is the universality of Mill's project (Gray 1996, p. 148). Rather than the logical expression of an empirical conception of human nature, or the empirical conclusion that modernization entails Westernization, Mill's liberal-utilitarian doctrine is, at best, a parochial expression of a European ideal of human flourishing. What is certainly undeniable is that modernity has in no significant way diminished the variety and depth of different cultural forms around the world. Globalization has perhaps made portions of the world more interdependent, but it has not brought with it a convergence on a form of life, and has even stimulated a resurgence of some ethnic and national identities. Even within the Western world, modernity has not diminished disputes over the limits of free speech, what the good life entails, or even foundational questions of social justice. If the value pluralism of Gray is true, then perhaps no one need attach any weight to Mill's unique projection of human flourishing. This rejection of progress would seem to be the only conclusion justifiable within Mill's empirical epistemology and inductive methodology. As Gray puts it, the status of Mill's project would be different "only if Mill were ready to forswear empiricism and nail his colours to the mast of an essentialist definition of man" (Gray 1996, p. 120). This concession would be beyond the pale for Mill. But his commitment to empiricism need not entail the abandonment of his project; his commitment to it only requires him to revise the project.

As Mill readily admits, his first principle of the value of happiness cannot be proved, and nothing discussed so far challenges that principle. What is being challenged is the strategy for maximizing it, and his presumption that there is ultimately only one. Mill is therefore right to construct his doctrine of reform on an empirical understanding of human nature. The sciences he employs have progressed tremendously since the mid-nineteenth century. Much more is known about the generic needs of humans and how these needs affect subjective measures of well-being. Most famously, Abraham Maslow proposes a hierarchy of basic needs ranging from the physiological requirements to the highest needs of self-actualization (Maslow 1943, p. 372). More recent research finds that such needs are not necessarily hierarchical as Maslow first argued, but confirms that the satisfaction of such universal and non-substitutable needs are necessary interests for any conception of human well-being (Tay, Diener 2011, p. 363). Perhaps more interesting for revising Mill's project, the work of Mihaly Csikszentmihalyi suggests that there is a generic human experience called optimal experience, or "flow," which seems akin to the higher pleasures. He describes it as "a particular kind of experience that is so engrossing and enjoyable that it becomes autotelic, that is, worth doing for its own sake even though it may have no consequence outside itself" (Csikszentmihalyi 1999, p. 824). Such research demonstrates that Mill was perhaps not so far off from what human nature requires and how it flourishes. If these needs can be quantified, then it might be possible to construct a framework for adjudicating between competing interests when attempting to maximize general well-being, and ultimately, happiness.

Whatever the status of the empirical grounding of Mill's doctrine, it is not as a scientist that his appeal endures. Mill was an eclectic and systematic thinker that articulated a novel (even if empirically unsustainable) vision of human flourishing that blends Romantic ideas about the infinite possibilities of the self with a rational methodology about how to realize these potentialities. Hence, some elements of this individualistic project will always transcend empiricism. His doctrine that connects the development of individuality to liberal principles has become a central strand in the varied tradition of liberalism, for both exponents and critics alike. Nonetheless, and in the spirit of Mill, it is necessary to question the reasons we have for holding Mill in such esteem, and to that end, to reexamine the evidence. The last thing Mill would want would be for his liberal-utilitarian doctrine to become yet another piece of "dead dogma."

NOTES

Chapter 2

1 Garforth, 1979, p. 30; Kenny, 1986, p. 2; Miller, 2010, p. 16.

2 Garforth, 1979, p. 31; Miller, 2010, p. 15.

3 For example, movies like Total Recall, Dark City, or Eternal Sunshine and the Spotless Mind.

4 Hamilton, 1998, p. 167; Donner and Fumerton, 2009, p. 158.

5 Ward, 1860, pp. 5–6, 25–9. Mill actually addresses Ward's critique in the Appendix to the first two chapters of *Examination*. Mill counters that any time there is a mental phenomenon that cannot be accounted for with experience, then we must accept it as intuitive. Where Mill and Ward disagree is over for what phenomena can be accounted. Mill claims that all mental phenomena except two—consciousness and memory—can be explained experientially.

6 Miller, 2010, p. 16; Donner and Fumerton, 2009, p. 168; Skorupski, 1998, p. 6.

7 For a longer discussion, see Haac, 1995. Mill discusses Comte's thought and influence in some detail. See Mill, 1969d, pp. 261–368.

8 The observation might wrongly identify an antecedent of an event in nature or in the mind, when in fact the antecedent and the event are really both consequents of a larger causal chain. Or, the observed relationship between an antecedent and a consequent can be broken down into more fundamental elements that might be involved in several other causal chains.

9 See Mill, 1969c, 212; Mill, 1963, p. 739. For a very comprehensive discussion of the historical development of Mill's thoughts on character formation, see Chapter Three of Carlisle, 1991.

10 See Carlisle, 1991, p. 161; Ball, 2000, 39.

Chapter 3

1 Push-pin was a child's game in the nineteenth century. Mill actually misquotes Bentham here. The full passage reads, "Prejudice apart, the game of push-pin is of equal value with the arts and sciences of music and poetry." See Jeremy Bentham (1843), "The Rationale for reward," in Collected Works, John Bowring (ed.). Accessed at http://www.laits.utexas.edu/poltheory/bentham/rr/

2 Plamenatz, 1966, p. 137; Riley 1999, p. 358.

3 For an alternative, Henry West proposes five broad steps. West, 2004, p.122

4 See also Mill, 1969e, "Nature," p. 377; West, 2004, p. 125; Crisp, 1997, p. 75; Dryer, 1969, p. lxxx.

5 Moore, 1962, p. 71. Crisp, 1997, p. 86; Dryer gives a justice based account of virtue: Dryer, 1969, p. xciii.

6 Berger relies on other essays and private correspondences. See Mill, 1972, p. 1319; Mill, 1967, p. 659; and Mill, 1967, p. 659.

7 See Dryer, 1969; Brown, 2010; Miller, 2010; Crisp, 1997; West, 2004; and Ryan, 1996.

8 In limiting punishment to moral condemnation, this interpretation follows Berger.

Chapter 4

1 There is a debate among scholars as to whether the liberty of expression is self-regarding, or if it really is other-regarding, but is considered self-regarding because there are good utilitarian reasons for considering it as such. See Riley, 1998, p. 75; and Riley, 2005.

2 For example, see Donner and Fumerton, 2009, pp. 62–8; Riley, 1998, p. 172; Ten, 1996, p. 234; Capaldi, 2004, p. 249.

3 The most infamous being Cowling, 1990; and Hamburger, 1999.

4 For example, see Kumar, 2010; Riley, p. 161, 1998; and Ten, 2002.

5 It is not obvious if Mill would allow for the prohibition on the public consumption of pork in a predominately Muslim country, in defense of *Islamic* good manners, or if Mill was fully dismissive of religiously derived sensibilities in the public domain.

Chapter 5

1 This oscillating conception of social evolution is captured by the positivist's motto "order and progress." The Brazilian flag has written on it "Ordem E Progresso," which is a tribute to the nation's positivitstic roots.

2 For example, see Cowling, 1990; Hamburger, 1999; and Raeder, 2002.

3 For example, see Miller, 2010, p. 189; and Thompson, 1976, p. 100.

4 Two attempts to reconstruct Mill's Religion of Humanity can be found in Hamburger, 1999; Raeder, 2002.

Chapter 6

1 Guardian Newspaper, 13 February 2008. The reprinting of the cartoon was in response to the thwarting of an alleged attempt to murder the cartoon's artist. This retributive aspect of the reprinting further questions the epistemological value of such expressions of free speech.

2 For a lively critique of Gray's thought by some of his many, critics, see John Horton and Glen Newey (eds.) (2007) The Political Theory of John Gray, (London: Routledge).

3 Gray rejects any notion of moral progress. His conclusion, derived from the fact of pluralism, is that the only terms of cooperation in society is a Hobbseian *modus vivendi*. See Gray, 2000.

BIBLIOGRAPHY

Works by Mill

Mill, J. S. (1965), 'Principles of Political Economy', in V. W. Bladen and
J. M. Robson (eds), *Collected Works III*. Toronto: Routledge and
Kegan Paul.

— (1967), 'Thorton On Labour and Its Claims', in L. Robbins and
J. Robson (eds), *Collected Works IV*. Toronto: Routlege Kegan and Paul.

— (1969a), 'Remarks on Bentham', in J. M. Robson (ed.), *Collected
Works X*. Toronto: Routledge and Kegan Paul.

— (1969b), 'Bentham', in J. M. Robson (ed.), *Collected Works X*. Toronto:
Routledge and Kegan Paul.

— (1969c), 'Utilitarianism', in J. M. Robson (ed.), *Collected Works X*.
Toronto: Routledge and Kegan Paul.

— (1969d), 'Auguste Comte and Positivism', in J. M. Robson (ed.),
Collected Works X. Toronto: Routlegde, and Kegan Paul.

— (1969e), 'Three Essays on Religion', in J. M. Robson (ed.), *Collected
Works X*. Toronto: Routledge, and Kegan Paul.

— (1969f), 'Coleridge', in J. M. Robson (ed.), *Collected Works X*.
Toronto: Routledge and Kegan Paul.

— (1972), 'Letter to Henry Jones', in F. Mineka and D. Lindley (eds).
Collected Works XVI. Toronto: Routledge and Kegan Paul.

— (1973), 'A System of Logic, Books I–III', in J. M. Robson (ed.),
Collected Works VII. Toronto: Routledge and Kegan Paul.

— (1974), 'A System of Logic, Books IV–VI', in J. M. Robson (ed.),
Collected Works VIII. Toronto: Routledge and Kegan Paul.

— (1977a), 'de Tocqueville on Democracy in America', in J. M. Robson
and A. Brady (eds), *Collected Works XVIII*. Toronto: Routledge and
Kegan Paul.

— (1977b), 'On Liberty', in J. M. Robson and A. Brady (eds), *Collected
Works XVIII*. Toronto: Routledge and Kegan Paul.

— (1977c), 'Considerations on Representative Government', in J. M.
Robson and A. Brady (eds), *Collected Works XIX*. Toronto: Routledge
and Kegan Paul.

— (1977d), 'Civilization', in J. M. Robson and A. Brady (eds), *Collected
Works XVIII*. Toronto: Routledge and Kegan Paul.

—(1979), 'An Examination of Sir William Hamilton's Philosophy', in J. M. Robson (ed.), *Collected Works IX*. Toronto: Routledge and Kegan Paul.

—(1981), 'Autobiography', in J. M. Robson and J. Stillinger (eds), *Collected Works I*. Toronto: Routledge and Kegan Paul.

—(1984a), 'The Subjection of Women', in J. M. Robson (ed.), *Collected Works XXI*. Toronto: Routledge and Kegan Paul.

—(1984b), 'Inaugural Address Delivered to St Andrews College', in J. M. Robson (ed.), *Collected Works XXII*, Toronto: Routledge and Kegan Paul.

—(1986), 'Spirit of the Age', in F. Mineka (ed.), *Collected Works XXII*. Toronto: Routlegde and Kegan Paul.

—(1988), 'Personal Representation' in J. M. Robson and B. L. Kinzer (eds), *Collected Works XXVIII*. Toronto: Routledge Kegan and Paul.

Other works

Ball, T. (2000), 'The Formation of Character: Mill's Ethology Reconsidered'. *Polity*, 32 (1), 25–48.

Beiser, F. C. (1992), *Enlightenment, Revolution, and Romanticism*. Cambridge, MA: Harvard University Press.

Berger, F. (1984), *Happiness, Justice, and Freedom*. Berkeley, CA: University of California Press.

Berlin, I. (1996), 'John Stuart Mill and the Ends of Life', in J. Gray and G. W. Smith (eds), *J. S. Mill On Liberty in Focus*. London: Routledge.

—(1998), 'Two Concepts of Liberty', in H. Hardy and R. Hausheer (eds), *The Proper Study of Mankind*. London: Pimlico.

Bentham, J. (1843), 'The Rationale for reward', in J. Bowring (ed.), *Collected Works*. Accessed at http://www.laits.utexas.edu/poltheory/bentham/rr/.

—(1970), in J. H. Burns and H. L. A. Hart (eds), *Introduction to the Principles of Morals and Legislation*. London: The Athlone Press.

Brown, D. G. (1972), 'Mill On Liberty and Morality'. *The Philosophical Review*, 81, (April), 133–58.

—(2010), 'Mill's Moral Theory: Ongoing revisionism'. *Politics, Philosophy and Economics*, 9 (1), 5–45.

Burrow, J. W. (1993), 'Introduction', in J. W. Burrow (ed.), *The Limits of State Action*. Cambridge: Cambridge University Press.

Capaldi, N. (2004), *John Stuart Mill*. Cambridge: Cambridge University Press.

Carlisle, J. (1991), *John Stuart Mill and the Writing of Character*. Athens: University of Georgia Press.

Carlyle, T. (2009), 'Sign of the Times', in G. Himmelfarb (ed.), *The Spirit of the Age*. New Haven: Yale University Press.

Comte, A. (1998), 'Plan of the Scientific Work Necessary for the Reorganisation of Society', in H. S. Jones (ed.), *Early Writings*. Cambridge: Cambridge University Press.

Coser, L. A. (1970), *Masters in Sociological Thought*. Fort Worth, TX: Harcourt Brace and Company.

Cowling, M. (1990), *Mill and Liberalism*. Cambridge: Cambridge University Press.

Crisp, R. (1997), *Mill on Utilitarianism*. London: Routledge.

Csikszentmihalyi, M. (1999), 'If We are so Rich, *Why aren't We Happy?*'. *American Psychologist*, 54 (10), 821–8.

Davidson, R. H., et al. (2011), *Congress and Its Members*. Washington D. C.: CQ Press.

Donner, W. (1991), *The Liberal Self: John Stuart Mill's Moral and Political Philosophy*. Ithica, NY: Cornell University Press.

Donner, W. and Fumerton, R. (2009), *Mill*. Chichester: Blackwell.

Dryer, D. P. (1969), 'Mill's Utilitarianism', in J. M. Robson (ed.), *Collected Works X*. Toronto: Routledge and Kegan Paul.

Dworkin, G. (1989), 'The Concept of Autonomy', in J. Christman (ed.), *The Inner Citadel*. Oxford: Oxford University Press.

Feinberg, J. (1984), *The Moral Limits of the Law: Vol. 1, Harm to Others*. New York: Oxford University Press.

Garforth, F. W. (1979), *John Stuart Mill's Theory of Education*. New York: Barnes and Noble.

Gray, J. (1995a), *Enlightenment's Wake*. London: Routledge.

—(1995b), *Berlin*. London: Fontana Press.

—(1996), *Mill On Liberty: A Defence*. London: Routledge.

—(1998), 'Where Pluralists and Liberals Part Company'. *International Journal of Philosophical Studies*, 6 (1), 17–36.

—(2000), *Two Faces of Liberalism*. New York: The New Press.

Gray, J. and Smith, G. W. (1996), 'Introduction', in J. Gray and G. W. Smith (eds), *J. S. Mill On Liberty in Focus*. London: Routledge.

Haac, O. A. (1995), *The Correspondence of John Stuart Mill and Auguste Comte*. New Brunswick: Transaction.

Habibi, D. (2001), *John Stuart Mill and the Ethic of Human Growth*. Dordrecht, NL: Kluwer Academic Publishers.

Hamburger, J. (1999), *John Stuart Mill on Liberty and Control*. Princeton, NJ: Princeton University Press.

Hamilton, A. (1998), 'Mill, Phenomenalism and the Self', in John Skorupski (ed.), *The Cambridge Companion to Mill*. Cambridge: Cambridge University Press.

Harrison, R. (1983), *Bentham*. London: Routledge and Kegan Paul.

Himmelfarb, G. (1974), *On Liberty and Liberalism*. New York: Alfred Knopf.

Honderich, T. (1982), 'On Liberty and Morality Dependant Harms'. *Political Studies*, 30 (4), 504–14.

Horton, J. and Newey, G. (eds) (2007), *The Political Theory of John Gray*. London: Routledge.

von Humboldt, W. (1993), in J. W. Burrow (ed.), *The Limits of State Action*. Cambridge: Cambridge University Press.

Hume, D. (1896), in L. A. Selby-Bigge (ed.), *Treatise on Human Nature*. Oxford: Oxford University Press.

Kenny, A. (1986), 'Introduction' in A. Kenny (ed.), *Rationalism, Empiricism, and Idealism*. Oxford: Clarendon Press.

Kumar, S. (2005), 'After Hamburger: The Revisionary Debate in Light of John Stuart Mill on Liberty and Control'. *Studies in Social and Political Thought*, 11, (May) 11–39.

—(2006), *Reassessing J. S. Mill's Liberalism: The Influence of Auguste Comte, Jeremy Bentham and Wilhelm von Humboldt*. London: LSE Doctoral Thesis.

—(2010), 'The Hierarchical Conception of the Self in On Liberty'.*The Mid South Political Science Review*, 11, 1–17.

Letwin, S. (1988), *The Pursuit of Certainty*. Indianapolis, IN: Liberty Fund.

Lijphart, A. (1999), *Patterns of Democracy*. New Haven, CT: Yale University Press.

Lyons, D. (1994), *Rights, Welfare and Mill's Moral Theory*. New York: Oxford University Press.

Macaulay, T. B. (1860), 'Mill on Government', in *The Miscellaneous Writings of Lord Macaulay, Vol. 2*. London: Longman, Green, Longman, and Roberts. Accessed from http://oll.libertyfund.org/title/99/48510.

Manuel, F. P. (1962), *The Prophets of Paris*. Cambridge, MA: Harvard University Press.

Maslow, A. H. (1943), 'A Theory of Human Motivation'. *Psychological Review*, 50 (4), 370–96.

Miller, D. E. (2010), *J. S. Mill*. London: Polity.

Moore, G. E. (1962), *Principia Ethica*. Cambridge: Cambridge University Press.

Morgan, G. (2007), 'Gray's Elegy for Progess', in J. Horton and G. Newey (eds) *The Political Theory of John Gray*. Oxford: Routledge.

Mueller, I. W. (1956), *John Stuart Mill and French Thought*. Urbana, IL: University of Illinois Press.

Pitkin, H. (1967), *The Concept of Representation*. Berkeley, CA: University of California Press.

Plamenatz, J. (1966), *The English Utilitarians*. Oxford: Basil Blackwell.

Raeder, L. C. (2002), *John Stuart Mill and the Religion of Humanity*. Columbia, MI: University of Missouri Press.

Rawls, J. (1999), *A Theory of Justice*. Cambridge, MA: Harvard University Press.

Raz, J. (1986), *The Morality of Freedom*. Oxford: Clarendon, 1986.

Rees, J. C. (1996), 'A Re-Reading of Mill's On Liberty', in J. Gray and G. W. Smith (eds), *J. S. Mill On Liberty in Focus*. London: Routlegde.

Riley, J. (1998), *Mill On Liberty*. London: Routledge.

—(1999), 'Is Qualitative Hedonism Incoherent?'. *Utilitas*, 11 (3), 347–58.

—(2005), 'J. S. Mill's Doctrine of Freedom of Expression'. in *Utilitas*, 17 (2), 147–79.

—(2007), 'Utilitarian Liberalism: Between Gray and Mill', in J. P. Horton and G. Newey (eds), *The Political Theory of John Gray*. Oxon: Routledge.

Roberts, J. (1984), 'T. H. Green', in Z. Pelczynski and J. Gray (eds), *Conceptions of Liberty in Political Philosophy*. New York: St Martin's Press.

Ryan, A. (1974), *J. S. Mill*. Boston: Routledge and Kegan Paul.

—(1996), 'John Stuart Mill's Art of Living', in J. Gray and G. W. Smith (eds), *J. S. Mill On Liberty in Focus*. London: Routledge.

Sandel, M. (1982), *Liberalism and the Limits of Justice*. Cambridge: Cambridge University Press.

Skorupski, J. (1998), 'Introduction', in J. Skorupski (ed.), *The Cambridge Companion to Mill*. Cambridge: Cambridge University Press.

Smith, G. W. (1991), 'Social Liberty and Free Agency', in J. Gray and G. W. Smith (eds), *J. S. Mill On Liberty in Focus*. London: Routledge.

Stephen, J. F. (1874), *Liberty, Equality and Fraternity*. London: Smith, Elder & Co.

Stocker, M. (1990), *Plural and Conflicting Values*. Oxford: Clarendon.

Tay, L. and Diener, E. (2011), 'Needs and Subjective Well-Being around the World'. *Journal of Personality and Social Psychology*, 101 (2), 354–65.

Ten, C. L. (1980), *Mill On Liberty*. Oxford, Clarendon.

—(1996), 'Mill's Defence of Liberty', in J. Gray, and G. W. Smith (eds), *John Stuart Mill on Liberty in Focus*. London: Routledge.

—(2002), 'Was Mill a Liberal?'. *Politics, Philosophy, & Economics*, l (3), 355–70.

Thompson, D. F. (1976), *John Stuart Mill and Representative Government*. Princeton, NJ: Princeton University Press.

Ward, W. G. (1860), *On Nature and Grace*. London: Burns and Lambert.

Wernick, A. (2001), *Auguste Comte and the Religion of Humanity*. Cambridge: Cambridge University Press.

West, H. R. (2004), *An Introduction to Mill's Utilitarian Ethics*. Cambridge: Cambridge University Press.

Whittaker, T. (1908), *Comte and Mill*. London: Archiblad Constable & Co Ltd.

Wilson, F. (1990), *Psychological Analysis and the Philosophy of John Stuart Mill*. Toronto: University of Toronto Press.

Wolff, J. (1998), 'Mill, Indecency, and the Liberty Principle', in *Utilitas*, 10 (1), pp. 1–16.

Wollheim, R. (1996), 'John Stuart Mill and Isaiah Berlin,' in J. Gray and G. W. Smith (eds), *John Stuart Mill On Liberty in Focus*. London: Routledge.

—(1999), 'The Limits of State Action', in C. L. Ten (ed.), *Mill's Moral, Political and Legal Philosophy*. Aldershot: Ashgate.

Wright, T. R. (1986), *The Religion of Humanity*. Cambridge: Cambridge University Press.

INDEX